ACOL BRIDGE FOR BRIGHT BEGINNERS

Are you lively-minded and have heard that bridge is now played by millions of equally lively-minded people around the world? And have you been thinking you also would like to play, but were concerned that learning the game might take up too much time? This book answers your problem. Written by Hugh Kelsey, international player, writer and critic and a leading world authority on bridge, and Andrew Kambites, a top bridge teacher and author, *Acol Bridge for Bright Beginners* is the ideal guide for you to learn about bridge.

A brief introduction showing how the game is played and the equipment you need is followed by clearly-explained chapters on bidding and on the play of the cards. Each chapter is backed up by carefully-designed quizzes so that you can test your progress and reinforce what you have learned.

Acol Bridge for Bright Beginners is bridge by the fast track, and in a remarkably short time you will be able to play and enjoy the excitement of this most challenging of card games.

D1354335

by HUGH KELSEY
in the Master Bridge Series

KILLING DEFENCE AT BRIDGE
SHARPEN YOUR BRIDGE TECHNIQUE
LOGICAL BRIDGE PLAY
TEST YOUR TIMING
TEST YOUR CARD PLAY: 3
TEST YOUR CARD PLAY: 4
MASTER SQUEEZE PLAY
MASTER PERCENTAGES IN BRIDGE
MASTER FINESSING
MASTER SLAM BIDDING
MASTER DOUBLES (*with Ron Klinger*)
ADVENTURES IN CARD PLAY (*with Géza Ottlik*)
BRIDGE ODDS FOR PRACTICAL PLAYERS (*with Michael Glauert*)
IMPROVE YOUR OPENING LEADS (*with John Matheson*)
INSTANT GUIDE TO STANDARD BRIDGE (*with Ron Klinger*)
ACOL BRIDGE FOR BRIGHT IMPROVERS (*with Andrew Kambites*)

* * *

by ANDREW KAMBITES

SIGNALS AND DISCARDS FOR YOU
CARD-PLACING FOR YOU
DEFENSIVE SKILLS FOR YOU

with Ron Klinger
BRIDGE CONVENTIONS FOR YOU
CARD PLAY MADE EASY 1: SAFETY PLAYS AND ENDPLAYS
CARD PLAY MADE EASY 2: KNOW YOUR SUIT COMBINATIONS
CARD PLAY MADE EASY 3: TRUMP MANAGEMENT
CARD PLAY MADE EASY 4: TIMING AND COMMUNICATION
HOW GOOD IS YOUR BRIDGE HAND?

with Eric Crowhurst
UNDERSTANDING ACOL

ACOL BRIDGE FOR BRIGHT BEGINNERS

Hugh Kelsey & Andrew Kambites

VICTOR GOLLANCZ
in association with
PETER CRAWLEY

Publishers' Note

Hugh Kelsey and Andrew Kambites had
completed and delivered the manuscript
of this book, and were at work on its
sequel, shortly before Hugh sadly died
early in 1995. The second book, *Acol
Bridge for Bright Improvers*, was
published in the Spring of 1996.

PSC

First published in Great Britain 1995
in association with Peter Crawley
by Victor Gollancz
an imprint of The Orion Publishing Group
Orion House, 5 Upper St Martin's Lane,
London WC2H 9EA

Second impression 2000

A catalogue record for this book
is available from the British Library

ISBN 0 575 06174 X

Photoset in Great Britain by
Rowland Phototypesetting Limited, Bury St Edmunds, Suffolk.
Printed in Great Britain by
Clays Ltd, St Ives plc.

Contents

Introduction

Your authors are saddened by the thought that some people manage to get through a lifetime without once playing a game of bridge. What a lot of pleasure they deny themselves.

The reasons for the rise in popularity of contract bridge, from its inception in 1925 to its present unchallenged position as the most widely played card game of all time, are numerous. Bridge has something for everyone.

Educationalists see bridge as offering a valuable social discipline, encouraging desirable traits, such as courtesy and communication skills. As an intellectual challenge bridge is unsurpassed, rewarding hard work and logical thought, and producing artistic beauty and elegance. You can play competitively, aiming to reach the top of the tournament circuit, or socially with friends in the comfort of your own home. Perhaps the greatest contribution of bridge to human happiness is the friendships it creates.

So what do you require to play bridge? Just three agreeable companions, a pack of cards and a few hours to while away. Bridge is a beguiling mixture of luck and skill, for while in the long run skill will prevail, in the short term there are those magic moments when the beginner gets the better of the expert.

If you have not yet tried bridge, it may be because you lack the confidence to make a start. The remedy is in your hands. This book is the passport to an exciting new world. Between the covers you will find all you need to enable you to take your place at the bridge table without fear of spoiling the game for your friends. We suggest you first read quickly through the book from beginning to end, skipping over any points that puzzle you. This will give you an overall picture, and you will discover that everything will fall into place when you go back for a second reading. This time take it slowly, chapter by chapter, demonstrating your progress by trying the quizzes at the end of each chapter, and checking your solutions against the answers at the back of the book. Ideally, you should supplement your reading with a little practice in the company of friends who are also beginners.

We confidently predict that you will soon share our enthusiasm, and you will have acquired a hobby to last you a lifetime.

1. Making a Start

Bridge is a game for four in which partners sit opposite one another with opponents to right and left. The game is played with an ordinary pack of cards from which the jokers have been removed. There are quite enough jokers among the players!

The Pack

The fifty-two cards in the pack are made up of thirteen cards in each of four suits. The suits are ♠ spades, ♡ hearts, ♢ diamonds and ♣ clubs. The cards in each suit rank from the ace (highest), king, queen, jack (or knave as it is sometimes called), and so on down to the two (lowest).

Tricks

In the play of the cards the objective is to win tricks. Each player in clockwise rotation places a card from his hand face upwards on the table. These four cards constitute a trick, which is won by the player who contributes the highest card of the suit led. There is an obligation on all players to 'follow suit'. This means that if the first player leads a spade, for instance, each of the other players must play a spade if he has one in his hand. Having no spades, a player may play any card he chooses.

In bridge diagrams it is convenient to use the cardinal points of the compass to designate the players. In the diagram on the next page only the heart suit is shown. North and South are partners against East and West. In this and other examples you will probably find it helpful to make up the suits from a pack of cards, setting up the cards in the diagram face up on the table, and turning over each card as it is played. This is easier than trying to keep track mentally.

Suppose West leads the ♡10 (ten of hearts), North plays the ♡6, East the ♡Q and South the ♡3. The ♡Q being the highest card, East wins the trick. He gathers the four cards and places them face downwards in a neat pile in front of him. Winning the trick gives a player the privilege of leading to the next trick, so in this case it is up to East to make the next lead.

At trick 2 he might continue with the ♡A, which will win the trick as the highest heart in the pack. Again East has to lead to trick 3. Suppose he perseveres with the ♡K. South and West must relinquish their last hearts and North cannot follow suit as he has no heart left. North must throw away (discard) a card from another suit and East wins the trick again. East can now win two more heart tricks because nobody else has a heart left.

Each player begins with thirteen cards and it follows that there are thirteen tricks to be won on every hand. The skill of card play lies in exploiting the potential of the partnership cards so as to win as many of the thirteen tricks as possible. In the above example East wins all the tricks, but West is content as it is the combined total of East and West tricks which will determine the East/West achievement.

Trumps

The highest card of the suit led will not always win the trick, for there may be a trump suit. This can be any one of the four suits which, in that particular hand, has precedence over the other suits. The trump suit is determined by the auction, as we shall see shortly, and it is a fact that a trump suit is present in most bridge hands.

Let us return to the heart suit on the previous page. You will remember that at trick 3 North could not 'follow suit', allowing East's ♡K to win the trick. However, suppose clubs were trumps. North, without any hearts left, would be free to play a club, perhaps the ♣2, which would win the trick. East can only grin and bear it.

Cutting for Partners

Let us go back for a moment to see exactly what happens when four players sit down at a bridge table. In the absence of any pre-arrangement it is customary to cut for partners. The pack is spread out face downwards on the table and each player draws a card. The players drawing the two highest cards play as partners against the other two. In the event of two players drawing cards of equal value, the ranking order of the suits decides the issue (spades rank highest, followed by hearts, diamonds and clubs).

The player who draws the highest card becomes the dealer and is entitled to two small privileges. He has the choice of seats (invaluable to those susceptible to draughts or superstitions) and also the choice of cards (it is convenient to play with two packs, although only one is used at a time).

Shuffle and Deal

The player on the dealer's left shuffles the cards and passes them face downward to his partner, who 'cuts' by taking a block of cards from the top of the pack and placing them closer to the dealer. The dealer completes the cut by placing the cards originally at the bottom of the pack on the top. He then deals out all the cards face downwards, one at a time, starting with the player on his left, continuing in a clockwise direction and finishing with himself. Meanwhile his partner shuffles the other pack and places it on his right, ready for the next deal.

When the deal is completed, the players pick up their cards and sort them into suits, taking care not to show their hands to the other players. It helps to hold the cards in a fan shape so you can see all thirteen cards at once.

Then the fun begins.

The Auction

To understand the purpose of a bridge auction simply reflect on how any other auction proceeds. Each interested party can make a bid, but nobody is compelled to do so. The highest bid wins the auction.

The dealer has the right to make the first bid. With a weak hand he may elect to pass by saying 'No bid', but with a strong hand he will certainly make a bid of some kind.

A bid at bridge is an undertaking that the partnership will win a stated number of tricks, either with a specified trump suit or with no trumps. Thus a bid of 'one club', or 1♣, is an offer to make seven or more tricks (adding six onto the one in 1♣) with clubs as trumps. A bid of 'three no trumps' or 3NT is a contract to take nine or more of the thirteen tricks without the benefit of any trump suit. The first six tricks are never mentioned in the auction.

As in any auction, the early bids are generally made at a low level. When the dealer has bid (or passed) it is the turn of the player on his left. (All the action at the bridge table takes place in a clockwise direction.) Each player in turn is entitled to bid, and the auction continues until no one is prepared to go any higher. The only rule is that each bid must be an advance on the previous bid. It must contract either for more tricks, or for the same number of tricks in a higher denomination. The ranking table reads as follows:

No trumps
Spades
Hearts
Diamonds
Clubs

The suits are in reverse alphabetical order, with no trumps outranking them all. Thus after a bid of 1♡ you may bid 1♠ or 1NT, but not 1♣ or 1◇. If you want to bid these suits you must go to the two-level, 2♣ or 2◇.

Below is a listing of the possible bids in order, starting with the cheapest.

1♣	1◇	1♡	1♠	1NT	2♣	2◇	2♡	2♠	2NT
3♣	3◇	3♡	3♠	3NT	4♣	4◇	4♡	4♠	4NT
5♣	5◇	5♡	5♠	5NT	6♣	6◇	6♡	6♠	6NT
7♣	7◇	7♡	7♠	7NT					

Now consider auction (i) below.

(i)

	SOUTH	WEST	NORTH	EAST
	1♣	1♠	2♣	2♠
	Pass	Pass	3♣	Pass
	Pass	Pass		

South deals and bids 1♣, promising that he (with the help of North's hand) will make 7 of the 13 tricks with clubs as trumps.

The next to bid is West. His 1♠ cancels South's 1♣ and contracts to make 7 tricks with spades as trumps.

It is now North's turn, and he chooses to outbid West in clubs. 1♣ isn't sufficient, so he must push the bidding up a level, to 2♣.

East then bids 2♠, South and West are content not to bid, but North decides to outbid East's 2♠ with 3♣. The other three players are allowed another bid, but each passes so the auction is ended. (If all four players had declined to bid at the start of the auction that would also end the auction, and with no contract made the cards would be redealt.)

The battle lines are now drawn. North/South have won the right to their chosen trump suit, but they must make at least 9 of the 13 available tricks. If they only make 8, they will have taken more than their opponents, but they will have reneged on their contract so they will score nothing and instead East/West will score points.

At the end of the auction a player with a special role must be identified. North's 3♣ won the auction, but the important thing is that a club bid won the auction and the first person on the 'auction winning' side to bid clubs was South. South becomes the *Declarer*.

At this stage it is worth considering why auction (i) might have developed. Clearly it is beneficial to each side to have a trump suit in which they have the majority of the cards. In auction (i) it is likely that North and South have most of the clubs, while East and West have most of the spades. North's 3♣ says that in his judgement his side will find it easier to take 9 tricks with clubs as trumps than to defeat the enemy contract of 2♠. He may well be right.

One side might try to outbid opponents in order to buy the right to their choice of denomination. However, it can make sense to outbid your partner, even in the same suit. Consider auction (ii).

(ii)	SOUTH	WEST	NORTH	EAST
	1♠	Pass	2♠	Pass
	4♠	Pass	Pass	Pass

At first sight the actions of North/South seem absurd, rather like a buyer outbidding himself or a member of his family in an auction. The answer lies in the method of scoring, which you will meet later.

If North/South promise to make 7 tricks and make 10 they score points, but if during the auction they contract to make 10 tricks and succeed they score bigger bonuses. It is clearly satisfying to succeed in your contract with tricks to spare, but if you consistently do this you are wasting the opportunity to score big bonuses.

Looked at in this light we try to interpret auction (ii). North's 2♠ says 'You have contracted to make 7 tricks with spades as trumps. I am confident you can make 8 tricks, and if you have extra strength there is a chance of the bonus for bidding and making 10 tricks.' South's 4♠ accepts the challenge.

Clearly North/South have the majority of the high cards and most of the spades.

The Play

When the auction has ended it is up to the defender on the left of the declarer to start the play. He makes the opening lead by placing one of his cards face upwards on the table.

As soon as the opening lead has been made, the declarer's partner lays his cards face upwards on the table. He should sort them neatly into suits, placing the trumps (if any) on his right. This is called the *dummy* hand. The declarer's partner, who is also referred to as dummy, takes no active part in the play of the cards. It is up to declarer to attempt to fulfil his contract by playing the cards from his hand and from dummy in proper clockwise rotation.

Of course this gives the declarer another advantage. He is the only player at the table who can see his partner's cards, let alone play them.

Scoring

We are not going to dwell on this at any great length, for scoring is best learned by experience. A full scoring table is given in appendix 2 but there are some basic features that you need to know from the start.

First, let us see what a score-pad looks like.

The vertical line down the middle separates the score of the goodies from the baddies. The middle horizontal line divides bonus points from trick points.

A rubber at bridge is the best of three *games*, and to make a game you need to score a total of 100 below the horizontal line. These points can be scored only by bidding

WE	THEY

and making contracts. Every time you succeed in a contract you score points for each trick (over six) that you make. The awards are as follows:

No-trumps: The first trick above six is worth 40 points and each subsequent trick is worth 30.

Spades/Hearts: Each trick above six is worth 30 points.
(the MAJOR suits)

Diamonds/Clubs: Each trick above six is worth 20 points.
(the MINOR suits)

The 100 points needed for game can be achieved on a single hand by bidding and making 3NT (40 + 30 + 30), 4♠ or 4♡ (4 × 30), or 5♢ or 5♣ (5 × 20).

Game may also be reached in stages, however. Suppose you play in a contract of 2♢ and make nine tricks. That scores 40 below the line towards game for 2♢ bid and made. The extra trick you made (known as an *overtrick*) is worth a further 20 points, but it is scored above the line and does not count towards game. Only those points that are *contracted for* and made are scored below the line.

Your 40 points below the line are known as a *part-score*. A further 60 points are needed for game, and you may well succeed in making up the balance on a later hand. If opponents score a game in the meanwhile, however, the contribution of your part-score towards a game is ended. A line is drawn right across the pad below the trick scores, and both sides start from scratch towards the next game.

Rubber Bonus

The pair that wins the rubber earns a big bonus, 700 points for a win by two games to nil and 500 for a win by two games to one.

Slam Bonuses

A contract for twelve tricks is known as a *small slam*, and a contract for all thirteen is known as a *grand slam*. Successful slams are rewarded by big bonuses, but there is little margin for error and until you gain experience we recommend caution.

Penalty Points

Just as there are rewards for making a contract so there are penalties for failure. Points are scored above the line by the defending side when they defeat a contract. The penalties depend on the state of the game.

If the declaring side has not yet made the first game towards rubber they are said to be NOT VULNERABLE. They concede 50 points for each trick by which their contract fails.

If the declaring side has won the first game towards rubber they are said to be VULNERABLE. They concede 100 points for each trick by which their contract fails.

The term 'vulnerable' is self-explanatory. A vulnerable pair is vulnerable to heavier penalties.

Double and Redouble

It may already have occurred to you that there could be times when it would pay to bid a contract that you know will fail, because the resulting penalty will be cheaper than allowing the opponents to fulfil their contract. This is indeed part of the game, but it is not as attractive as it might seem.

If a player considers that his opponents have bitten off more than they can chew, he may say 'double' when it is his turn to bid. The effect, if the contract fails, is to increase the penalty substantially, particularly if declarer is vulnerable.

If the contract succeeds in spite of a double, the trick score is doubled and the declarer receives a bonus of 50 points above the line. A contract of 2♡ doubled and made, for example, would give the declarer a game, scoring 120 below the line and 50 above.

There is a further point that when you double, either of your opponents may redouble if he considers that the contract will be made. The redouble increases yet again the rewards of success and the penalties of failure.

Like any other call, a double or redouble ends the auction when it is followed by three passes. A further bid by one of the three players, however, has the effect of cancelling the double (or redouble) and keeping the auction alive. Here is a possible auction:

SOUTH	WEST	NORTH	EAST
1♡	Pass	4♡	Double (i)
Pass	Pass	Redouble (ii)	Pass
Pass	4♠ (iii)	Double (iv)	Pass
Pass	Pass		

(i)   East thinks he can beat 4♡.
(ii) North disagrees.
(iii) West takes fright, thus cancelling the previous double and redouble.
(iv) North is out for blood.

Honours

The ace, king, queen, jack and ten are known as *honour cards*. If a player holds all five trump honours in one hand he is entitled to a bonus of 150 points above the line. Four trump honours in one hand are worth 100 points. And in a no-trump contract, holding all four aces is worth 150 points. Claim these bonuses at the end of the game.

Settling up

When the rubber ends the scores for each side, above and below the line, are totted up and the difference calculated to the nearest 100. It is normal to play for a stake (however small) to prevent a whimsical opponent bidding 7NT on every deal just to have the pleasure of playing the hand. The losers pay the winners at the agreed rate per hundred, and the next rubber commences.

The scorecard of a possible (if rather exciting) rubber is shown in appendix 2.

2. The Principles of Good Bidding

We have seen that the purpose of bidding is to arrive at a contract that suits the combined values of the partnership hands. This is not the haphazard process is might seem at first glance. Good players don't just guess. They have a method for calculating how strong a hand is, and a *system* for deciding what to bid.

Evaluating a Hand

For the purpose of valuing high cards in your hand a simple point count is used.

Each ace counts 4 points.
Each king counts 3 points.
Each queen counts 2 points.
Each jack counts one point.

There are 40 points in the pack, and an *average* hand has 10 points.

Remember that these points are counted solely in the bidding and have nothing to do with the scoring points used in the last chapter.

High-card points alone do not fully demonstrate the trick-taking capabilities of your hand. Suppose you have all 13 spades. This comes to only 10 points, yet clearly you can underwrite a grand slam in spades. The key to this is your *length* in spades. You have seen a rather less extreme example of this on page 10 where East's ♡4 and ♡2 could score tricks because they were the only hearts left.

If you intend to bid a suit, rather than no-trumps, add length points to the hand's value as follows:

A 5-card suit counts one point.
A 6-card suit counts 2 points.
A 7-card suit counts 3 points.
Each additional card in a suit counts one extra point.

Let us see how it works on this hand:

♠ 9
♡ K Q 8 5 3 2
♢ A 7 2
♣ A 10 4

There are 13 high-card points (HCP): two aces at 4 each, one king at 3 and one queen at 2. There are also 2 length points for the six-card heart suit. Total: 15 points. This gives an accurate initial estimate of the potential of the hand, rather better than average.

We would now like to introduce you to some bridge terminology that describes the shape of a hand.

If you have three cards in a suit, that is called a *tripleton*.

If you have two cards in a suit, that is called a *doubleton*.

If you have only one card in a suit it is called a *singleton*.

If you have no card in a suit you are said to be *void* in that suit.

When you pick up a hand you should count the points, and then determine the *shape* of the four suits. You would describe the hand above as having 1–6–3–3 shape with 13 high-card points, or 15 total points.

Using the Point Count

When reading chapter 1 you may have realised the desirability of bidding and making a game contract on a single deal if your cards are good enough, before your opponents wipe out your part-score with their own game.

The table below lists the cheapest game contracts, and shows why spades and hearts are known as 'major suits', while diamonds and clubs are the 'minor suits'.

3NT (40 + 30 + 30) = 100
4♡ or 4♠ (30 × 4) = 120
5♣ or 5♢ (20 × 5) = 100

Bidding theory assumes you don't have a part-score. If you do have a part-score you should use common sense to adapt. For example, with no score below the line you might risk 3NT, accepting the possibility of failure. This would be unnecessary if you already had a part-score of 60 because bidding and making 1NT with overtricks would be just as good as bidding and making 3NT. A good rule of thumb is to underbid by one trick if you already have a part-score.

So, assuming we have no part-score already, how do we know whether to contract for part-score or game?

The generally accepted criterion is that if your side has a combined 25 points you attempt game (though as 28 points tends to be desirable for 5♣ or 5♢ players tend to prefer to play in 3NT or a major suit game if such an alternative is reasonable). We are not promising that you will make your game contract, merely that in view of the tempting rubber bonuses you should take the risk if your chances of success are as high as 50%. You shouldn't be worried at bidding borderline game contracts and sometimes failing. The opposite is true. *If you never fail in a game contract, you are underbidding and therefore not using the full potential of your cards.*

Equally, if you want a rough guide for bidding slams, 34 points generally makes a small slam playable while 37 points should make you consider a grand slam.

Good bidding revolves round seizing game opportunities. It would be foolish for both partners to pass out a hand if game is possible. That makes it necessary for a player with 13 points to make a bid, because if both partners pass with 13 points, a combined 26 might be wasted.

♠ Q 9 7 4 3
♡ A K
♢ 8 5
♣ Q J 3 2

This hand has 12 HCP and one length point, and should be opened 1♠, spades being the *longest* suit. Admittedly you have the best of your high cards in hearts, but the point to grasp is that your ♡A K will score tricks whatever the trump suit. The point of suggesting spades as trumps is that your little spades will score tricks if they are trumps when nobody has any spades left. Of course you cannot guarantee the 7 tricks you are contracting for, indeed if partner is very weak you may have no chance. However, you must assume partner has a little something, otherwise life becomes impossible.

The player who first makes a bid is called the *opener*. Opener's 1♠ shows 12–19 points. It doesn't make sense for him to jump to 2♠ with, say, 16 points just to show that he has a bit more. Opener and his partner (called *responder*) may need a discussion (through the bidding) to determine which is the best trump suit, or indeed whether a trump suit is necessary. This is known as settling the *denomination*. Each discussion point pushes the auction higher, and the art of good bidding is to determine the best denomination at a low enough level to succeed.

Suppose opener starts with 1♠, the next player passes, and it is responder's turn.
 1♠ showed 12–19 points. If responder has as few as 6 points the partnership may have a combined 25 points, so he should aim to bid, allowing for the possibility that opener is very strong. The partners have embarked on a process which will end with a final contract that is sound in two ways:
  (i)   The denomination chosen must be sensible.
  (ii) The level (game, part-score or slam) must be realistic.

Choosing the Denomination

When you select a trump suit you need to hold more cards in that suit than the enemy, preferably at least eight. The partners can gradually tell each other how many cards each holds in a suit which they are considering as a possible trump suit as follows:

(i) To introduce a suit to the auction you need at least four cards in that suit. The quality shouldn't matter, though it is often recommended that beginners shouldn't introduce a very weak 4-card suit.

Thus if partner opens 1♠ and you have four spades you know that your side has at least an 8-card spade fit. You know that, but partner doesn't, so it is your responsibility to ensure that spades are trumps.

(ii) If partner doesn't support your suit, bidding your suit a second time shows at least a 5-card suit. Thus if partner bids and rebids spades and you have three spades you know of an 8-card spade fit, so spades will be trumps.

Of course, sometimes the partners bid different suits and no 8-card 'fit' emerges. Now is the time to consider a no-trump contract, particularly since 3NT is the cheapest game. Indeed, if an 8-card minor suit fit comes to light the players might choose to ignore it and settle in 3NT, nine tricks being easier than eleven. You will find most bidding focuses on finding a major suit fit, or exploring the feasibility of playing no-trumps.

Playing in no-trumps makes sense if the hands are *balanced*, with no particularly long or short suits. Short suits tend to be a problem in no-trump contracts because the defenders will quickly force out your high cards (stoppers) and on regaining the lead they will score length tricks with tiny cards in the suit. Trump contracts are desirable when there is length and strength in one suit and corresponding weakness and shortage in another. The trump suit prevents defenders from running riot by cashing winners in declarer's weak suit.

Choosing the Level

Suppose South opens 1♡ (12–19 points) and North responds 1♠ (6+ points). As yet the partners may still have no idea of the likely level or denomination. The breakthrough usually comes when one of the players makes a *Limit Bid*. This is a bid which narrows his point range, usually to within 2 or 3 points. For example, consider the auction below with neither side having a part-score:

SOUTH	WEST	NORTH	EAST
1♡	Pass	1♠	Pass
1NT	Pass	?	

Later you will learn that a rebid of 1NT shows 15–16 points, and a balanced hand. South has already promised 4 hearts, so North (the member of the partnership with the greatest knowledge of his partner's hand) should know what to do. North might have any of these hands:

(a)	♠ A J 3 2	(b)	♠ A J 8 5 4 3	(c)	♠ A Q 9 3
	♡ 6 4		♡ 9		♡ 9 3
	◇ 9 5 4		◇ 8 5 2		◇ Q 9 6 5
	♣ K 10 7 5		♣ J 10 7		♣ K 8 5

North knows that:
(1) South hasn't got four spades, otherwise he would have supported spades rather than rebidding no trumps.
(2) South has a balanced hand, no singleton or void.

With (a) North concludes that the partnership has 23 or 24 points, not enough for game, and fewer than 8 spades. 1NT seems a sensible contract. Note that he doesn't wonder whether a bigger part-score below the line may be possible. Having given up on game he terminates the auction as quickly as he can, by passing.

With (b) North works out that there is not enough for game, and that the partnership has at least 8 spades. He bids 2♠, ending the auction.

With (c) North knows that there is no suitable spade fit, and the combined point total is 26 or 27, so game values are present. North closes the auction with a jump to 3NT.

It is important for you to understand the logic of this. One player describes his hand accurately, the other uses his common sense to determine the final contract.

Fits and Misfits

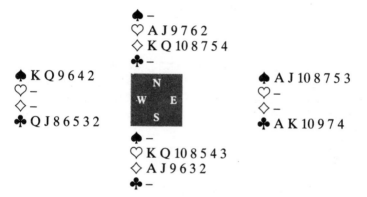

♠ –
♡ A J 9 7 6 2
◇ K Q 10 8 7 5 4
♣ –

♠ K Q 9 6 4 2
♡ –
◇ –
♣ Q J 8 6 5 3 2

♠ A J 10 8 7 5 3
♡ –
◇ –
♣ A K 10 9 7 4

♠ –
♡ K Q 10 8 5 4 3
◇ A J 9 6 3 2
♣ –

This deal is somewhat freakish, but it illustrates well that even after adding on length points the point count can give a very inaccurate assessment of trick-taking potential.

North/South have 20 HCP. They can make 7♡ or 7◇.

East/West have 20 HCP. They can make 7♠ or 7♣.

Understanding why is the key to good bidding. The point here is that each side has a wonderful *fit*. If your partner bids hearts and you have lots of hearts you have a good fit. Bid aggressively! Not only might you make your contract, but your opponents might make a high-level spade contract given the chance.

It is equally instructive to look at what happens when partnership hands misfit. In the next diagram we have taken our previous hand and swapped the South and West cards. Can you work out who can make what?

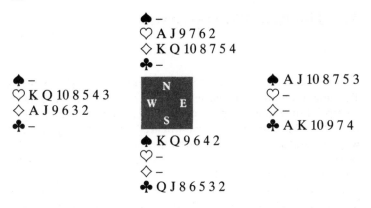

♠ –
♡ A J 9 7 6 2
♢ K Q 10 8 7 5 4
♣ –

♠ –
♡ K Q 10 8 5 4 3
♢ A J 9 6 3 2
♣ –

♠ A J 10 8 7 5 3
♡ –
♢ –
♣ A K 10 9 7 4

♠ K Q 9 6 4 2
♡ –
♢ –
♣ Q J 8 6 5 3 2

Difficult isn't it! One thing is certain. Whichever player first gets into the bidding is likely to find himself in a battle royal with his partner. By the time the bidding subsides the auction will be far too high, and it is likely than an opponent will double gleefully.

The time is not yet right for us to discuss the bidding of this hand, which possibly is just as well for we could not honestly claim that we would emerge intact from this horror. This is a very difficult hand, and we only include it to demonstrate the danger inherent in a misfit. Rather than discuss this we will take a more ordinary situation. How do you rate the next hand:

(i)   if partner opens 1♡?
(ii) if partner opens 1♠?

♠ –
♡ K 10 8 4 3 2
♢ 8 4
♣ 10 9 7 4 3

This hand will make lots of tricks opposite a 1♡ opening bid. You will learn that it is worth jumping to 4♡ despite the low point count. Opposite a 1♠ opening the alarm bells should sound. Probably each side has a misfit, and it might be wise to pass before matters get worse.

3. The Acol Bidding System

As you may have seen, bids contain a hidden message. Opener's 1♡ might mean, 'I promise to take 7 tricks with hearts as trumps', but responder interprets it as a coded message saying, 'I have 12–19 points and at least 4 hearts'. A bidding system is a way of co-ordinating these coded messages. The most popular system in Britain and many other countries, and the system we are teaching you, is called, ACOL.

The key to understanding Acol is to realise that most bids can be classified into various types. We will illustrate some of these bids by referring to an auction we have already discussed.

SOUTH	WEST	NORTH	EAST
1♡	Pass	1♠	Pass
1NT	Pass	2♠	All Pass

Limit Bids

The limit bid is the most distinctive feature of Acol. A player makes a bid which very closely defines his hand strength, leaving partner to use common sense to decide upon the correct contract. In the above auction South's 1NT rebid is a limit bid, showing a balanced hand with 15–16 points.

Most Acol auctions feature a limit bid by the second round of bidding. The following are usually limit bids:
(i)   No trump bids.
(ii) Support of partner's suit.
(iii) A rebid of your own suit.
That doesn't leave much does it? Just the bid of a new suit.

Wide-Ranging Bids

A wide-ranging bid is the opposite of a limit bid. For example, South's 1♡ opening covers the range 12–19 points. Clearly responder cannot be expected to pick the final contract until much more information has been exchanged.

Forcing Bids

Suppose opener starts with 1♡ and you, responder, have:

♠ A J 7 3 2
♡ J 8 4
♢ Q 8 4
♣ A Q

Clearly you want to reach at least a game contract, however as yet you cannot choose between 3NT, 4♡, 4♠, or even a slam if opener is very strong. You want to show your spades by responding 1♠ and hear a second bid from partner, but you need reassurance that partner will not pass just because he has a minimum opening bid. Unless the opponents intervene your 1♠ response *forces* him to bid again.

Forcing bids can be divided into two categories:
(a) *Forcing for One Round*
The 1♠ response to 1♡ forces opener to find a rebid, but not necessarily a third bid. With the hand shown responder intends to make sure game is reached, but the 1♠ bid could have concealed just 6 HCP, making it necessary that the bidding die quickly unless opener has great strength.
(b) *Game-Forcing*
Some bids make an unconditional demand that the bidding be kept open until game is reached. Where such a bid is available the partnership clearly has plenty of space to discuss the final contract.

Sign-off Bids

North's 2♠ said that he was convinced that this was the best contract and *demanded* that South pass, called a sign-off. Predictably a sign-off bid often follows a limit bid.

Invitational Bids

Usually if partner makes a limit bid you can decide between game or part-score without further ado. However, sometimes you want further clarification within the narrow limits he has set.

If you have a balanced hand with 12 HCP and partner opens 1NT (which shows 12–14 HCP) you want to play in game only if he is at the upper end of this range. You can bid an *invitational* 2NT, asking him to reassess his hand *in the context of what he has already shown*. Note that a hand with 14 HCP isn't good or bad in itself. If you have shown 12–14 HCP and partner is still interested in game, 14 HCP is very encouraging. But if you had shown 14–16 HCP, then 14 HCP is minimum.

Conventional Bids

There are those who prefer to play totally natural bridge, where a club bid always shows clubs. However most players choose to replace the natural meaning of some bids by an artificial meaning, generally because that is more useful. Such a bid is called a *conventional* bid. For example, playing Acol all exceptionally strong hands are opened 2♣, whether or not the hand has a club suit. 2♣ is used purely as a way of creating a game-forcing auction.

From now onwards we use the following abbreviated notation to classify bids:

[L]   Limit bid
[WR]   Wide-ranging bid
[F]   Forcing bid
[F1R]   Forcing bid for one round
[GF]   Game-Forcing bid
[NF]   Not forcing
[S]   Sign-off bid
[I]   Invitational bid
[C]   Conventional bid

A good way of practising your bidding is to deal hands and bid them with a friend, stating the classification of each bid as you make it. Our sample auction might go as follows:

South: 'One heart, wide ranging, not forcing.'
North: 'One spade, wide ranging, forcing one round.'
South: 'One no-trump, limit bid.'
North: 'Two spades, sign-off.'

Opener has a Balanced Hand

By now you might think that if opener has at least 13 points he picks a suit with at least four cards to bid. It isn't that simple! Suppose you as dealer open 1♡ with:

♠ 9 6 5
♡ A K Q J
♢ 9 4 3
♣ K 10 6

Partner is quite likely to respond 1♠ [F]. What then?
You cannot pass as 1♠ is forcing.
You cannot rebid 1NT [L] as that shows 15–16 points.
You cannot rebid 2♡ [L] as that shows at least five hearts.
You cannot raise to 2♠ [L] because partner will think you have 4-card support.
　You are stuck!
　The problem is that you opened 1♡ with no thought as to your rebid, and it is now too late. Common advice is to have a rebid ready to use over any possible forcing response. This is good advice, but rather demanding. There is a simpler way. Opener starts by classifying his hand shape as *balanced* or *unbalanced*.

A *balanced* hand can have one of the following shape patterns: 4–3–3–3, 4–4–3–2 (or sometimes 5–3–3–2).
　Thus a balanced hand has no singleton or void, and at most one doubleton.
　If opener has a balanced hand he should aim to show it with a no-trump bid, either on his opening bid or on his rebid if responder changes suit. This doesn't give him any leeway for making a mistake on the first bid.
　A 1NT [L] opening bid shows 12–14 points. With 12–14 points and a balanced hand opener *must* open 1NT because all no-trump rebids show a stronger hand than 14 points. Thus with the hand above the correct opening bid was 1NT even though it contains no honour card in spades or diamonds. Of course it would be nice to have the honour cards evenly distributed between the suits, but it is far more important to show your hand-type as quickly as

possible. Note that opening 1NT doesn't necessarily commit you to a no-trump contract. Armed with the precise knowledge offered by a limit bid responder may choose a superior suit contract.

We now consider balanced hands with more than 14 points. The following table shows the strength of no-trump rebids.

No-trump rebid	Points needed after a one-level response	Points needed after a two-level response
1NT [L]	15–16	
2NT [L]	17–18	15–16
3NT [L]	19	17–19

So how does opener handle these hands?

(a)   ♠ 6 3 2   (b)   ♠ Q 10 2
        ♡ A K Q J   ♡ A K Q J
        ◇ K 7 3   ◇ K 7 3
        ♣ K 4 2   ♣ K 4 2

With (a) he opens 1♡ (his only 4-card suit) and plans a 1NT rebid if responder bids 1♠, or a 2NT rebid if responder bids 2♣ or 2◇.

With (b) he opens 1♡ and plans a 2NT rebid if responder bids 1♠, or a 3NT rebid if responder bids 2♣ or 2◇.

Don't worry that a higher level rebid is necessary after a 2♣ or 2◇ response. You will learn later that a two-level change of suit promises more points than a one-level response, making the higher rebid safe.

How about unbalanced hands? All unbalanced hands have at least one 5-card suit except those with 4–4–4–1 shape. Therefore if opener chooses to show an unbalanced hand shape by bidding two suits there is a strong indication that his first suit is likely to have at least five cards.

Opener has an Unbalanced Hand

With an unbalanced hand opener plans to bid two suits or bid and rebid his suit.

(c)   ♠ 4   (d)   ♠ Q J 7 6 5
       ♡ A Q 9 7   ♡ K Q J 6 3
       ◇ A 8   ◇ 4
       ♣ Q 8 6 4 3 2   ♣ K 2

He should open his *longest* suit. 1♣ is correct with (c). At this stage he should pessimistically assume that responder will bid diamonds or spades, one of his short suits. In that event he would like to rebid in his second suit, hearts. Rebidding 1♡ is easy if the response is 1◇ [F], but a 2♡ rebid after a 1♠ [F] response would be uncomfortably high. With a minimum opening bid opener does have some responsibility for keeping the bidding low, particularly since responder could have just six points. He should rebid 2♣ over a 1♠ response.

With (d) opener clearly wishes to bid both suits, and it is the question of which order makes more economical use of bidding space. 1♠ may be the more expensive start, but a rebid of 2♡ over a response of 2♣ [F] or 2◇ [F] is cheaper than opening 1♡ and rebidding 2♠. A recurring theme is that *with a minimum opening bid opener should not rebid in a higher ranking suit at the two-level than the suit he opened.* The solution here is that if you are dealt two 5-card suits you should open the higher.

(e)   ♠ Q J 7 6 5   (f)   ♠ Q J 7 6 5
       ♡ 4   ♡ 4
       ◇ K Q J 6 3   ◇ K 2
       ♣ K 2   ♣ K Q J 6 3

Opening 1♠ with (e) doesn't solve all problems. If the response is 2♣ [F] you will be happy to rebid 2◇, but over a 2♡ [F] response you are too weak to raise the bidding to 3◇, leaving you with an ugly but unavoidable 2♠ rebid.

Hand (f) is the exception to the rule of opening the higher of 5-card suits. With clubs and spades open 1♣, intending a 1♠ rebid over 1♢ [F] or 1♡ [F].

(g)   ♠ A K 6 4   (h)   ♠ A K 6 4
        ♡ A J 5 3   ♡ A J 5 3
        ♢ 8   ♢ A 9 4 2
        ♣ A 9 4 2   ♣ 8

If your unbalanced hand does not contain a 5-card suit it must have three 4-card suits and a singleton.

Hand (g) has a red suit singleton. You are safe if you open the *suit below the singleton*, in this case 1♣. You plan to rebid 1♡ if the response is 1♢ [F].

Hand (h) has a black suit singleton. Best is to open the *middle* of the three touching suits, 1♡. If partner responds 1♠ [F] you will be delighted to support his suit, but over the more likely 2♣ [F] response you will rebid 2♢.

(j)   ♠ A K 6 4   (k)   ♠ A K 6 4
        ♡ A J 5 3   ♡ A J
        ♢ 8 4 2   ♢ A 9 4 2
        ♣ A 9   ♣ 8 5 3

Hands (j) and (k) are balanced, but they are too strong for a 1NT opening bid. You must therefore plan to rebid no-trumps at an appropriate level, but in the meantime you must open a suit.

Hand (j) is instructive. If you intended to bid both suits it would undoubtedly be best to open 1♠, allowing an economical 2♡ rebid. However, you only intend to bid one of them, and in that case it makes sense to bid the one that makes it easier for responder to introduce the other. If you open 1♡ he can easily respond 1♠ if he has four spades, otherwise you rebid 2NT. Open the *lower* of touching 4-card suits if your hand is balanced.

With (k) you can open 1♢ or 1♠, again intending a no-trump rebid. We recommend 1♠ because it is more important to investigate a major fit than a minor fit.

Quiz 1

For each of the following hands:

(i)   state your opening bid.

(ii)   if you choose to open with a suit bid state your planned rebid if partner responds with any of the suits in which you don't have four cards.

a)   ♠ A J 8
     ♡ 9 6 2
     ◇ K J 6 3
     ♣ A 9 7

b)   ♠ A J 8
     ♡ K 6 2
     ◇ K J 6 3
     ♣ A 9 7

c)   ♠ A J 8
     ♡ K 6 2
     ◇ K J 6 3
     ♣ A K 9

d)   ♠ A J
     ♡ K 6 2
     ◇ Q 8 4 3 2
     ♣ K 9 7

e)   ♠ K 4
     ♡ A J 8 3
     ◇ K Q 9 2
     ♣ 10 4 3

f)   ♠ K 4
     ♡ A J 8 3
     ◇ K Q 9 2
     ♣ A 4 3

g)   ♠ 4 2
     ♡ K J 8 3 2
     ◇ A J 10 2
     ♣ K 7

h)   ♠ A J 10 2
     ♡ K J 8 3 2
     ◇ 4 2
     ♣ K 7

i)   ♠ K 3
     ♡ K J 6 3 2
     ◇ A J 5 3 2
     ♣ 9

j)   ♠ K 3
     ♡ K J 6 3 2
     ◇ 9
     ♣ A J 5 3 2

k)   ♠ A J 8 4 3 2
     ♡ K J 5 3
     ◇ K 8
     ♣ 10

l)   ♠ K J 5 3
     ♡ A J 8 4 3 2
     ◇ K 8
     ♣ 10

m)   ♠ 2
     ♡ K J 8 2
     ◇ J 8 3 2
     ♣ A K 9 3

n)   ♠ K J 8 2
     ♡ 2
     ◇ J 8 3 2
     ♣ A K 9 3

p)   ♠ K J 8 2
     ♡ J 8 3 2
     ◇ 2
     ♣ A K 9 3

4. Responding to 1NT

Sign-off Bids

Because 1NT is a limit bid, responder often finds it easy to pick the final contract, hence most responses are sign-off bids.

2♦, 2♡ and 2♠ show 0–10 points and at least a 5-card suit. Responder does not necessarily expect to make his contract, he simply prefers it to 1NT. He would sign off in 2♠ with:

♠ Q 10 8 5 4 3
♡ 8 4
♦ 6
♣ J 8 4 3

3NT shows 13–19 HCP and a balanced shape.

4♡, 4♠, 5♣ and 5♦. Responder has at least a 6-card suit and sufficient values for game, 13+ points.
    Responder would bid 4♠ with hand (a) below.

6♣, 6♦, 6♡, 6♠ or 6NT. Responder knows what opener has and considers the bid slam to be best.

Game-Forcing Bids

3♣ and 3♦ show at least a 5-card suit. Responder will often prefer 3NT if only interested in game because nine tricks are easier than eleven, so he will have slam interest.
    3♡ and 3♠ show precisely a 5-card suit and game values. Responder doesn't know whether 3NT or 4♡/♠ is best. Opener is expected to raise to four of the major with 3-card or 4-card support, or rebid 3NT with just doubleton support.
    Responder would bid 3♠ with hand (b).

(a)	♠ A Q J 7 4 3	(b)	♠ A J 7 4 3
	♡ 9		♡ K 9
	♦ K J 6		♦ K J 6
	♣ Q 9 4		♣ Q 9 4

Invitational Bids

2NT shows a balanced hand with 11–12 HCP. Responder is still interested in game if opener is maximum for his 1NT opening bid. Opener raises to 3NT with 14 HCP, passes with 12 HCP and if he has 13 points he raises if his hand has a bit extra, e.g., a ten.

4NT shows 20 HCP and invites opener to bid 6NT if he has a maximum.

The obvious omission in our list is 2♣. You can use it as a sign-off, just like 2◇/♡/♠, but it is common to give it a conventional use. See appendix 1 for further information.

Quiz 2

1) Your partner opens the bidding with 1NT. Give your response with these hands and state its classification.

a)	♠ K J 2	b)	♠ K J 2	c)	♠ K J 2
	♡ Q 8 2		♡ Q 8 2		♡ A 8 2
	◇ K 9 4		◇ K 9 4		◇ K 9 4
	♣ J 8 3 2		♣ K 8 3 2		♣ K 8 3 2

d)	♠ 9 6	e)	♠ 9 6	f)	♠ 9 6
	♡ J 10 8 4 3 2		♡ A J 8 4 3 2		♡ A J 8 4 3
	◇ 9 6		◇ A Q		◇ A Q 2
	♣ Q 8 3		♣ Q 8 3		♣ Q 8 3

2) With the following hands you open 1NT. What is your rebid after each of the responses below?

a)	♠ K J 2	b)	♠ K J	c)	♠ K J 2
	♡ Q 10 9		♡ A 10 9 2		♡ A 10
	◇ A 8 3		◇ A 8 3		◇ A 8 3 2
	♣ Q 9 3 2		♣ Q 9 3 2		♣ Q 9 3 2

(i) 2♡   (ii) 2NT   (iii) 3♡   (iv) 3NT   (v) 4♡

5. Responding to Suit Bids

You will find it easier to grasp the structure of responses to a suit opening bid if you understand the order of doing things. Firstly, you must settle the denomination (suit or no-trumps). Then you determine the level. There is not enough bidding space available to jump about to show a strong hand when you have no idea of the denomination.

Responder Supports Opener's Suit

Opener has shown at least a 4-card suit, so if responder has 4-card support the search for the right denomination is over before it has begun. The only problem concerns the level at which you should play. Responder can make a limit bid to suggest the level, jumping if necessary.

After a 1♡ [WR] opening bid responder supports his partner's suit according to the table below.

2♡ [L]   shows 6–9 points and 4+ hearts, hand (a).
3♡ [L]   shows 10–12 points and 4+ hearts, hand (b).
4♡ [L]   shows 13–15 points and 4+ hearts, hand (c).

(a)	♠ K J 7	(b)	♠ K J 7	(c)	♠ K J 7
	♡ Q 10 6 5		♡ Q 10 6 5		♡ Q 10 6 4
	◇ 9 5 3 2		◇ A 5 3 2		◇ A K 3 2
	♣ 10 6		♣ 10 6		♣ 10 6

Note the values 6–9 and 10–12. They constantly recur.

You should be prepared to bid even more aggressively if you have a good fit with partner and great shape.

(d)	♠ 9 7 3 2	(e)	♠ 9
	♡ Q 10 6 5		♡ K 10 6 5 3
	◇ –		◇ 10
	♣ 9 6 5 3 2		♣ A 8 6 5 3 2

With hand (d) raise 1♡ to 2♡ [L], expecting to make tricks by ruffing diamonds.

With (e) jump to 4♡ [L]. 4♡ will probably make, and just as important, 4♠ may well make for your opponents. It is good tactics to make it hard for opponents to bid at a safe level. Such an attempt to bully opponents out of their dues is called *pre-emptive bidding* and you will meet it again later.

If you want a more methodical way of valuing your hand when supporting partner, try discounting length points and instead counting shortage points: 5 for a void, 3 for a singleton and one for a doubleton. That makes hand (d) worth 7 points, and hand (e) worth 13 points.

Since these raises are limit bids opener's common sense will probably tell him what to do next. Suppose opener's 1♡ is raised to 2♡ [L] and he holds these hands.

(f)	♠ K J 7	(g)	♠ K Q 7	(h)	♠ K J 7
	♡ A Q 8 3		♡ A Q J 7 3		♡ A Q J 7 3
	◇ A 9 2		◇ A Q J 8		◇ A 9 8 4
	♣ J 10 6		♣ 4		♣ 6

With (f) he intended a no-trump rebid, but new information has come to light, namely that responder has 6–9 points. No game is likely, so there is no point in bidding on.

With (g) he knows the correct contract is 4♡. There appears to be a 9-card heart fit and the combined point count is at least 26. He closes the auction with 4♡ [S].

With (h) he is still unsure as to whether game or part-score is correct. He could pass this message with 3♡ [I]. The logic is inescapable. With no interest in game he would have passed, while if he knew game was desirable he would have bid it. Therefore he wants responder to proceed with 8–9 points, but not with 6–7. A better bid still is the *trial bid* of 3◇ [F], showing a second suit and helping responder to judge how good is the fit between the two hands. He will place greater value on the ◇K or ◇Q than the ♣K or ♣Q.

Responder bids No-trumps

If you raise opener's suit the trump suit is agreed. If instead you respond in no-trumps the denomination is not so clear, but since you are suggesting a balanced hand partner should be well-placed to decide. Hence it is sensible to determine that no-trump responses are limit bids.

If opener starts with 1♡ [WR]:

1NT [L] shows 6–9 points, hand (a).
2NT [L] shows 11–12 points, balanced, hand (b).
3NT [L] shows 13–15 points, balanced, hand (c).

(a)	♠ K 8 3	(b)	♠ K 8 3	(c)	♠ K Q 3
	♡ 7 2		♡ 7 2		♡ 9 7 2
	◇ Q 10 7 2		◇ Q 10 7 2		◇ Q 10 7 2
	♣ K 6 4 3		♣ A Q 9 2		♣ A Q 9

Each of these bids denies four hearts (otherwise it would be appropriate for responder to support opener's suit), or four spades (a 4-card major that could be shown at the one level). Once again there is a great premium on finding a 4–4 major suit fit if one exists.

Two questions may have occurred to you.

Firstly, how about a balanced hand with ten points? Yes, there is a gap, which is solved by changing suit [F1R] and rebidding 2NT, which then shows 10–12 points.

Secondly, why is the word 'balanced' missing from the 1NT response? Consider hands (d) and (e). Both are rotten, misfitting hands, hardly suitable for a forcing and space-consuming change of suit at the two level. Improvising a 1NT [L] response is the least ugly bid. You will learn that a perfect bid is not always available, making compromise necessary.

(d)	♠ K 9 3	(e)	♠ A 2
	♡ 8		♡ 2
	◇ K 9 6 4 3		◇ K 9 6 4 3
	♣ 10 7 4 2		♣ 10 9 7 4 2

After a 1NT [L] response to 1♡ [WR] opener can bid game directly, or alternatively he can:

(i)   rebid his suit at the two level, 2♡ [S], but he needs at least a 6-card suit to do so, hand (f).
(ii) jump rebid his suit, 3♡ [I], hand (g).
(iii) bid a new suit at the two level, 2♣ [NF], hand (h).
(iv) raise to 2NT [I], hand (i).
(v)   jump in a new suit, 3♣ [GF], hand (j).

(f)	♠ K 7 2	(g)	♠ K 7
	♡ A Q 9 6 4 3		♡ A Q 9 6 4 3
	◇ Q 4 2		◇ A Q 2
	♣ J		♣ J 7

(h)	♠ Q 7 2	(i)	♠ K 7 2	(j)	♠ A J 2
	♡ A Q 9 6 3		♡ A Q 9 6		♡ A Q 9 6 3
	◇ 7		◇ A J 4		◇ 7
	♣ A J 4 2		♣ K J 10		♣ A K J 4

After a 2NT [L] response to 1♡ [WR] opener can:
(i)   bid game directly, for example 3NT with hand (k).
(ii) rebid his suit at the three level, 3♡ [S], hand (l).
(iii) introduce a new suit, 3♣ [F], hand (m).

(k)	♠ Q 7 2	(l)	♠ Q 7 2	(m)	♠ Q 7 2
	♡ Q J 8 3 2		♡ A Q J 9 3 2		♡ A Q 9 6 3
	◇ A Q 8		◇ Q 8 5		◇ 9
	♣ A Q		♣ 9		♣ A K 9 2

Responder Changes Suit

If opener bids 1♡ [WR]:
(i)   A new suit by responder at the one level (i.e., 1♠ [F1R] [WR]) shows 6+ points and 4+ spades.
     Respond 1♠ with (n), (p) or (q).

(n)	♠ K 9 6 2	(p)	♠ A Q 7 2	(q)	♠ A Q 8 4 3 2
	♡ 9 8		♡ K 6 5		♡ K 6
	◇ Q J 4 3		◇ K 9		◇ K 9
	♣ 10 7 2		♣ K 8 4 2		♣ J 7 3

(ii) A new suit by responder at the two level (i.e., 2♣/♢ [F1R] [WR]) shows 8+ points and 4+ clubs/diamonds.

The extra strength required is logical because it doesn't make sense to push the bidding high with a weak hand. Even 8 and 9 point hands are only worth changing suit at the two level if responder has a little something in opener's suit. If in doubt respond 1NT [L] [NF], as with (d) and (e).

After 1♡ from opener, respond 2♣ with (r) and (s).

(r) ♠ A 8   (s) ♠ A K J
     ♡ 8 5 2   ♡ 10
     ♢ 10 6 3   ♢ K 7 5 2
     ♣ A J 10 6 4   ♣ Q 9 6 4 3

Note that while it is sometimes necessary to respond to 1♠ with 2♣ or 2♢ [F] on a 4-card suit, a 2♡ [F] response in reply to 1♠ promises at least 5 hearts.

(iii) A jump in a new suit by responder (i.e., 2♠/3♣/3♢ [GF]) shows 16+ points. Most experts play that it promises at least a 5-card suit, but that shouldn't worry you yet.

After 1♡ from opener, jump to 3♣ with (t), (u) or (v).

Holding (t) you intend to support hearts on the next round, showing heart support and a club suit.

With (u) you will repeat your clubs to show a truly excellent suit.

If you have (v) you can follow up with 3NT to show 16 or 17 points and a club suit.

(t) ♠ 8 4 -   (u) ♠ 8 4   (v) ♠ K 8 5
     ♡ K J 7 3   ♡ K 7   ♡ K 7
     ♢ A 5   ♢ A 5 2   ♢ A 5 2
     ♣ A K J 7 2   ♣ A K J 10 3 2   ♣ A Q 7 5 2

The advantage of making an immediate jump in a new suit (known as a *jump shift*) is that having described your strength and forced to game you can subsequently bid cheaply and naturally, secure in the knowledge that partner will not drop the bidding until game is reached.

Choice of Suit

For the responder, the choice of suit is determined by three simple guidelines.

(1) With suits of unequal length, bid the longest.

(2) With two 5-card or longer suits, bid the higher ranking. That keeps the bidding cheaper when you rebid the other suit, the logic being the same as that governing opening the higher of two 5-card suits.

(3) With nothing but 4-card suits, bid your cheapest suit.

Consider your response on these hands opposite opener's 1♢.

(w) ♠ Q 9 5 3 2   (x) ♠ K J 4 2
    ♡ K J 4 2   ♡ J 7
    ♢ J 7   ♢ J 6
    ♣ J 6   ♣ Q 9 5 3 2

(y) ♠ K 8 3 2   (z) ♠ K J 4 2
    ♡ Q 9 4 3   ♡ Q 9
    ♢ J 5   ♢ A J 6 3
    ♣ K 8 4   ♣ 6 3 2

With (w) bid 1♠ [F], but (x) is an exception to guideline (1). This hand is barely strong enough for 2♣ [F], and since your priority is to find a major suit fit, respond 1♠. You don't like starting with your shorter suit, but the principle of bidding cheaply with a weak hand makes compromise necessary. Make the hand a little stronger, for example replacing the ♡J by the ♡A, and you should start with your longer suit, 2♣ [WR] [F1R].

Hands (y) and (z) also demonstrate the special status of the major suit.

With (y) respond 1♡ [F] (the lower of your two 4-card major suits), even though you have an ideal no-trump hand. That way you won't miss a 4–4 heart of spade fit. A 1NT response would deny a 4-card major suit that could have been shown at the one level.

With (z) respond 1♠ [F] rather than jump to 3♢ [L]. Prefer to explore a major fit before agreeing a minor.

Quiz 3

1) Give your response with the following hands after each of the opening bids listed below. State the classification of your bid.

a) ♠ 8 4 3
♡ K 4 2
◇ A Q 3
♣ Q 8 4 2

b) ♠ Q 8 4 2
♡ K 4 2
◇ A Q 3
♣ 8 4 3

c) ♠ 8 7
♡ J 10 8 4
◇ A 10 9 8 4
♣ J 3

d) ♠ A 7
♡ J 10 8 4
◇ A 10 9 6 4
♣ J 7

e) ♠ Q 10 2
♡ A 8
◇ A Q 10 8 4
♣ K Q 4

f) ♠ A 10 9 6 4
♡ Q 10 8 4
◇ 8 7
♣ 9 3

g) ♠ 2
♡ K 9 4 3 2
◇ K 8 4 3 2
♣ 10 6

h) ♠ A Q 6 2
♡ K 9 3 2
◇ 4
♣ 9 6 4 3

j) ♠ –
♡ Q 9 8 5 4 3
◇ K J 7 2
♣ 8 4 3

(i) 1♣   (ii) 1◇   (iii) 1♡   (iv) 1♠

2) With each of the following hands you open 1♠. What is your rebid after each of the responses below? State the classification of your bid.

a) ♠ A Q 8 3 2
♡ A 5
◇ K J 7
♣ 9 6 3

b) ♠ A Q J 4 3
♡ A J 2
◇ K 7 3 2
♣ 9

c) ♠ A J 9 4 3 2
♡ A K 2
◇ K Q 7
♣ 4

(i) 2♠   (ii) 3♠   (iii) 1NT   (iv) 2NT

6. Opener's Rebid

We have already considered opener's continuation if responder makes a limit bid. Now we examine his rebid if responder changes suit. The principle is similar to that governing responder's actions, namely a rebid in no-trumps or in a suit that has already been bid is a limit bid.

Opener Rebids No-trumps

This has already been dealt with on page 31.

Opener Supports Responder's Suit

If opener starts with 1◇ and responder bids 1♡:

    2♡ [L]   shows 12–15 points and 4+ hearts.
    3♡ [L]   shows 16–18 points and 4+ hearts.
    4♡ [L]   shows 19–20 points and 4+ hearts.

There is less space available after a two-level response so the values change slightly.

If opener starts with 1◇ and responder bids 2♣:

    3♣ [L]   shows 12–16 points and 4+ clubs.
    4♣ [F]   shows 17+ points and 4+ clubs. It is logical that
4♣ should be forcing if opener has 17+ and responder 8+.

After 1♠ Pass 2♡ Pass opener can raise hearts with just 3-card support as the 2♡ response guarantees a 5-card suit.

Opener Rebids his Own Suit

If opener rebids his own suit this is a limit bid. The higher the level, the more powerful the suit needs to be.

If opener starts with 1♡ and responder bids 1♠, 2♣ or 2◇:

    2♡ [L]   shows 12–15 points. At least 5 hearts.
    3♡ [L]   shows 16–18 points. At least 6 hearts.
    4♡ [L]   shows 18–19 points. At least 7 hearts.

The types of problem faced by opener are best understood by looking at some hands. In each case the opening bid was 1♡ and 1♠ was responded.

(a)	♠ 9 6	(b)	♠ K 6	(c)	♠ K 6
	♡ K J 9 8 4		♡ K J 9 8 4		♡ K Q J 9 8 4
	◇ A Q 9		◇ A Q 9		◇ A 10 4
	♣ K 6 2		♣ K J 2		♣ K 2

With (a) opener would like to rebid no-trumps, but a 1NT [L] rebid would show 15–16 points. Therefore he must rebid 2♡ [L], which shows his fifth heart and point count.

With (b) opener is too strong for a 2♡ [L] rebid, and lacks the sixth heart and suit quality for 3♡ [L]. A jump to 2NT [L] is best, accurately showing his point count and relatively balanced shape, though responder won't know about the fifth heart.

With (c) opener has the perfect hand for a 3♡ [L] rebid.

Opener Introduces a Third Suit

The auction tends to become a little more complicated if opener bids a third suit because such a bid covers a very wide point range. Suppose opener starts with 1♡ and hears a 1♠ response. He rebids 2◇ [WR] [NF] with (d) or (e), showing 12–18 points. He needs 19 points to jump in a new suit, 3◇ [GF], hand (f). 3◇ is called a *jump shift*.

(d)	♠ 9	(e)	♠ 9	(f)	♠ 9
	♡ A J 8 4 3		♡ A K J 8 3		♡ A K J 8 3
	◇ K Q 7 2		◇ K Q 7 2		◇ A K 7 2
	♣ Q 10 9		♣ A 10 9		♣ A 10 9

Opener had no difficulties with these hands because diamonds is a lower ranking suit than hearts, making the 2◇ rebid economical. There is more of a problem with the next three hands. In each case opener starts with 1♡, his longest suit, and has to find a rebid over 2◇.

(g) ♠ K Q 7 2　　(h) ♠ K Q 7 2　　(i) ♠ K 10 9
　　♡ A J 8 4 3　　　♡ A K J 8 4　　　♡ A K J 8 4
　　◇ 9　　　　　　　◇ 9　　　　　　　◇ 9
　　♣ Q 10 9　　　　♣ K 10 9　　　　♣ K Q 7 2

With (g) opener is too weak to by pass 2♡, and should content himself with rebidding his 5-card suit, 2♡ [L].

With (h) opener has the values to show his second suit even though it means by-passing his first suit. Rebidding 2♠ is called a *reverse*. It shows longer hearts than spades, at least 16 points and is forcing.

With (i) opener can reverse into 3♣ [F]. This shows shape as well as strength (at least 16 points). Opener has at least five hearts, and might also hold five clubs.

Quiz 4

With each of the following hands you open 1◇. What is your rebid after each of the responses below? State the classification of your rebid.

a) ♠ K 3　　　　b) ♠ A 3　　　　c) ♠ A 3
　 ♡ 9 7 2　　　　 ♡ J 7 2　　　　 ♡ 8 6
　 ◇ A Q J 6 2　　 ◇ A Q J 6 2　　 ◇ A Q J 9 6 3
　 ♣ K 6 3　　　　 ♣ K 6 3　　　　 ♣ 9 4 2

d) ♠ A 3　　　　e) ♠ K J 7 2　　f) ♠ K Q 7 2
　 ♡ A 6　　　　 ♡ K 5 2　　　　 ♡ A J
　 ◇ A Q J 9 6 3　◇ A J 9 6 3　　 ◇ A Q 9 6 3
　 ♣ 9 4 2　　　　♣ 9　　　　　　 ♣ 9 2

g) ♠ K 4　　　　h) ♠ 6　　　　　j) ♠ 6 2
　 ♡ K J 9 6　　　 ♡ A 7　　　　　 ♡ 7 2
　 ◇ A J 8 2　　　 ◇ A J 9 6 3　　 ◇ A K 9 6 3
　 ♣ A 9 3　　　　 ♣ Q 9 8 3 2　　 ♣ A K Q 2

(i) 1♡　　　(ii) 1♠　　　(iii) 2♣

7. Responder's Rebid

By now we can only hope to consider a sample of the possibilities. You will get most decisions right if you work on the principle that most bids by responder on the second round show the same values as they would have shown on the first round.

We can give you one important word of advice. If you can see that game is unlikely you should stop bidding as soon as you conveniently can. It is losing bridge to keep pushing up the level of the auction in the hope that an elusive fit may appear. If you have a combined 20 points it is better to play in 2♡ on a 7-card fit than in 3NT (probably doubled). If you are not convinced, refer back to page 26 to see the potential horrors of a misfit.

If three suits have been bid, the bidding has reached the two level, and responder is weak he has three choices. Suppose the auction starts like this.

SOUTH	NORTH
1♡	1♠
2♢	?

(a)	♠ K J 7 4 3	(b)	♠ K J 7 3 2	(c)	♠ K Q 10 9 7 6
	♡ 9		♡ 9 2		♡ 2
	♢ 7 3 2		♢ 7 3		♢ 7 3
	♣ K 10 3 2		♣ Q 7 3 2		♣ Q 7 3 2

Responder can pass. With (a) he cannot be sure that 2♢ is best, but it is reasonable. He cannot bid 2NT to show his club stopper because that shows 10–12 points.

Responder can go back to opener's suit at the lowest legal level. With (b) he rebids 2♡. He wants to terminate the auction quickly, and however imperfect a contract of 2♡ is it will surely be preferable to 2◇. Hearts is opener's first suit, and he will either have longer hearts than diamonds or the same length. Returning to partner's first suit at the lowest level shows no additional strength, and is known as giving *simple preference*.

Responder can repeat his own suit at the lowest legal level, but he needs a good 6-card suit for this. With hand (c) he rebids 2♠. Note that the spade suits in (a) and (b) are not of sufficient quality for 2♠.

Any of these rebids is quite likely to lead to a 7-card fit. When the combined hands are sufficiently strong to play in game you can continue bidding long enough to discover the best denomination, usually an 8-card fit if you choose a trump suit. You cannot afford this luxury if you have less combined strength. The priority is to come to rest in a sensible, if not perfect, contract at a low enough level to give you a reasonable chance of success.

Quiz 5

You respond 1♠ [F] [WR] to your partner's opening 1♡ with these hands. Try logically to work out your next move after each of the rebids shown below.

a)   ♠ A 9 8 5   b)   ♠ A J 6 3 2   c)   ♠ K J 6 3
     ♡ Q 6 2   ♡ J 7 3   ♡ 7 3
     ◇ 10 5   ◇ K 8   ◇ K 8 6
     ♣ 10 9 5 3   ♣ Q 10 6   ♣ Q J 10 2

d)   ♠ A J 10 9 6 3   e)   ♠ A J 10 9 4 3
     ♡ 2   ♡ 2
     ◇ 9 8   ◇ A 9 8
     ♣ 10 9 4 3   ♣ J 10 6

(i) 1NT   (ii) 2◇   (iii) 2♡   (iv) 2♠   (v) 2NT   (vi) 3♠

8. Strong Opening Bids

The Opening 2♣ Bid

They say it is better to be lucky than good. We are not in a position to comment on your virtue, but we can guarantee you sometimes will be lucky enough to hold a hand that is too strong for an opening bid of one-in-a-suit, a hand that will produce game even if partner contributes nothing but a shapeless collection of junk.

♠ A K Q 10 2   ♠ 3
♡ A K J 8 3   ♡ 10 6 5 2
♢ A J   ♢ 9 7 3 2
♣ 6   ♣ 10 8 7 3

If you hold the West hand you can be fairly confident of making game in one of the major suits, but which one? Spades are your stronger suit but you can hardly open 4♠ in case partner has the East hand. Equally you cannot open 1♠ in case partner passes. You need to buy a little time to investigate the best contract, and you do this by making a conventional opening bid of 2♣. This says nothing about your clubs. It just tells partner to keep open the bidding at all costs until game is reached. Thereafter West can bid naturally, confident that partner will not pass.

After a 2♣ [C] opening responder gives a 'negative' conventional response of 2♢ if he holds less than eight points (or seven if he has an ace and a king). 2♢ warns opener not to get too excited. Any other bid would be natural and show positive values, at least seven points. The bidding may then continue as shown below, West starting with the higher ranking of his suits, East keeping the ball rolling with 2NT and West introducing his hearts.

WEST	EAST
2♣	2♢
2♠	2NT
3♡	4♡

Having given a negative response of 2◇, the responder need not be reluctant to show a 5-card suit on the next round of bidding, for example:

♠ A Q 8 7 4 3   ♠ 2
♡ A K 6   ♡ Q J 7 5 2
◇ A K Q   ◇ 9 5 4
♣ 3   ♣ 10 8 4 2

WEST	EAST
2♣	2◇
2♠	3♡
4♡	

4♡ is by far the best contract, but it cannot be reached unless East bids the suit.

We now need to define more closely the requirements for an opening bid of 2♣. The big hands fall into two categories.
1)   Distributional hands with upwards of 20 HCP and an expectancy of taking at least nine tricks if partner can give no help.
2)   Balanced hands containing at least 23 points. After opening 2♣ on a balanced hand, you rebid 2NT [L] with 23–24 points, or 3NT [L] with 25–27. The rebid of 2NT is not forcing if the response was 2◇, after all a balanced hand with 23–24 points doesn't expect to make game if partner is completely worthless. This is the one exception to the rule that an opening 2♣ is game-forcing.

Opening Two Bids in Other Suits

Hands that are almost, but not quite, good enough to force to game may be opened with bids of 2♠, 2♡ or 2◇, called *Acol Two* bids. These bids promise at least eight tricks in the opening hand and are forcing for one round only.

The opener's hand may be either single-suited, or two-suited and the normal point range is from 14 to 19. An Acol Two opening bid promises a good suit, certainly at least A Q J 3 2 or A J 9 4 3 2. If responder has 3-card support then he should have no worries about making it the trump suit. With either (a) or (b) open 2♠.

(a)   ♠ A Q J 9 8 7 2   (b)   ♠ K Q 10 8 6 2
      ♡ 7   ♡ 4
      ◇ A K 8   ◇ A Q 10 9 5
      ♣ 9 2   ♣ A

The negative response to an Acol Two bid is 2NT (again showing less than 8 points). Logically any other response is game-forcing.

When responding to an Acol Two bid you should try to imagine whether your cards are likely to be of use to partner. In the hand below East might appear to have rubbish, but his ♠J, 3-card spade support and ◇K must be wonderful news opposite a partner with spades and diamonds.

♠ K Q 10 8 6 2   ♠ J 9 5
♡ 7   ♡ 10 8 4 2
◇ A Q 10 9 5   ◇ K 6
♣ A   ♣ 8 4 3 2

WEST	EAST
2♠	2NT
3◇	4♠

Note that East would have been far less impressed if he had been dealt the ♡Q and ♣Q instead of the ♠J and ◇K, since they would be useless opposite West's shortage. East would then have bid only 3♠ over 3◇, which West could pass.

If you are starting to see that as the auction develops some high cards are more useful than others, you are showing signs of the judgement that separates the expert from his less distinguished opponent.

The Opening 2NT Bid

This shows a balanced hand with 20–22 HCP. There is less room for investigation than over a 1NT opening, which means that you cannot sign off in a part-score. 3◇/♡/♠ [GF] show 5-card suits and, if you wish, you can use 3♣ as the Stayman convention described in appendix 1.

A 2NT opening bid may not always be as balanced as one would like. What else can you bid with these hands?

♠ A Q   ♠ A Q
♡ K J 8 3   ♡ K 10 6
♢ A Q   ♢ K 3
♣ A J 5 3 2   ♣ A K Q 5 3 2

Quiz 6

1) What do you open with these hands? If your bid is forcing, state your rebid over partner's conventional weak response and classify your rebid.

a) ♠ K 8 4 3 2   b) ♠ K Q 4 2   c) ♠ A Q J 7 5
   ♡ A J 7   ♡ A J 7 6   ♡ K Q J 9 6
   ♢ A K 9   ♢ A K 9   ♢ A 8 5
   ♣ A Q   ♣ A Q   ♣ –

d) ♠ A K J 7 5   e) ♠ A Q J 9 7 4   f) ♠ Q 9 6 5 3
   ♡ A K Q 9 6   ♡ 9   ♡ A K Q 10
   ♢ A Q 5   ♢ K Q J   ♢ 5
   ♣ –   ♣ A J 8   ♣ A K Q

2) Below are three hands. For each one decide what you would bid as North after the following sequences.

a) ♠ Q J 6   b) ♠ A 9 7 4 3   c) ♠ Q 10 7
   ♡ 8 6   ♡ 9 7 5   ♡ 9 3
   ♢ 9 7 4 3   ♢ 10 7   ♢ 9 8 4
   ♣ 8 5 3 2   ♣ 8 4 2   ♣ A 9 8 4 3

(i) SOUTH NORTH   (ii) SOUTH NORTH   (iii) SOUTH NORTH
    2♣   2♢   2♣   2♢   2♡   2NT
    2NT   ?   2♡   ?   3♡   ?

9. Bidding a Slam

There is nothing in bridge to equal the thrill of bidding and making your first slam. Large bonuses are awarded for successful slams (see the scoring table in appendix 2), making the venture profitable as well as supremely satisfying. A slam that fails represents a sure game lost, however, damaging your finances and your morale.

The chance of a slam will come your way roughly once in every twenty deals, but you should not attempt them all. Contracting for twelve or thirteen tricks is a risky business, and we suggest that while you are finding your feet at bridge you should only bid those slams that appear sure to succeed. Don't worry if you find yourself making twelve tricks when you have bid no higher than game. It does not pay to be too ambitious.

The time to consider a slam is when you become aware of considerable excess strength, over and above that needed for game, in the combined hands. A positive response to 2♣ opening bid suggests that you are close to the slam zone. So does a jump in a new suit by responder when opener has a better than minimum opening bid, or a jump rebid by the opener when responder has the values for an opening bid.

Common Sense Slam Bidding

West		East
♠ A Q 9 4		♠ K J 6
♡ K J 8		♡ Q 10 6
◇ A K 2		◇ Q 8 4 3
♣ K J 2		♣ A Q 6

East and West should bid a slam using simple common sense.

If West is dealer he will open 2NT. East has 14 points, making at least a combined 34, the requirement for a slam with a balanced hand. Without further ado he jumps to 6NT.

If East is dealer he opens 1NT. West wants to be in 6NT unless East has a minimum 1NT, so he jumps to 4NT [I]. With 14 HCP East is happy to trust his partner and bid 6NT.

The Blackwood Convention

If you add your partner's announced HCP total to your own and the total is at least 34 points you are not worried that the opponents may start cashing two aces. However on distributional hands with a good trump fit a slam may be made with considerably less than 34 points. Suppose you open 2♣ [C] with the hand below, and partner responds 2♢ [C]. You rebid 2♠ [GF], and are delighted to hear him raise to 3♠.

♠ K Q J 10 6 3 2
♡ A K
♢ 6
♣ A K Q

Partner wouldn't have responded 2♢ with two aces, but so long as he was one ace 6♠ will surely make, and if he has no ace 5♠ can hardly fail. You really are not interested in other missing cards, you simply want to know how many aces he has. When a trump suit has been firmly agreed there is a conventional way of asking how many aces he has. You can use a jump to 4NT [C] [F] as the Blackwood convention. He is expected to reply as follows:

5♣ = no ace or four aces.
5♢ = one ace.
5♡ = two aces.
5♠ = three aces.

When you hear the answer you will set the final contract. If you decide 5♠ is correct, partner *must not* raise to 6♠. You have assumed the captaincy of the partnership for the duration of the auction.

Blackwood is such a simple convention, and such fun to use that you may be tempted to give it an airing on unsuitable occasions. Do not use it unless you are sure the strength for a slam is present, and do not use it unless you have agreed a trump suit.

Be particularly wary of using Blackwood when your suit is a minor. If your suit is clubs, for instance, you cannot afford to bid 4NT with only one ace in your hand. If partner also has one ace his response of 5♢ will take you too high.

Blackwood is best regarded not as an aid to slam bidding, but as a means of keeping out of bad slams.

When the response to 4NT confirms that all the aces are present you may, if interested in a grand slam, continue with a bid of 5NT [C] to ask for kings. The responses are on a similar schedule.

6♣ = no king.
6♢ = one king.
6♡ = two kings.
6♠ = three kings.
6NT = all four kings.

Cue-Bidding

How do you continue with the South hand shown below after the shown start to the auction?

♠ A K 8 7 3	SOUTH	NORTH
♡ A K Q 5 3	1♠	3♠
♢ 9 7 3	?	
♣ –		

Your hand has a lot of playing strength, and you would like to try a slam, but there is a danger that the opponents will start by cashing the ♢ A K. Using Blackwood and finding partner with one ace won't help, the ♣A being useless. The answer is to bid 4♣, a *cue bid*. When the trump suit has been agreed the bid of a new suit at a high level shows *control* of the suit, the ace or a void. You are saying you can take the first trick if they lead a club. If partner cue-bids 4♢ you can confidently jump to 6♠.

Don't worry about cue bids yet, but bear in mind you will probably find them useful one day.

Quiz 7

1) What is your third bid with these South hands after the auction shown below?

SOUTH	NORTH
1♣	1♠
2♠	4NT
?	

a) ♠ Q J 8 2
♡ A 6
♢ J 2
♣ A J 9 8 3

b) ♠ Q J 8 4
♡ A 9 4
♢ 9
♣ K Q 8 3 2

c) ♠ A 9 7 4
♡ A 6
♢ J 2
♣ A 10 8 4 2

d) ♠ K 9 4 2
♡ K 6
♢ J 2
♣ K Q J 8 3

2) How do you continue with these North hands after the auction shown below?

SOUTH	NORTH
2♣	2♠
3♣	?

a) ♠ K J 8 4 2
♡ 9 8 3
♢ A 8 2
♣ 10 6

b) ♠ A J 9 5 4
♡ K 8 3
♢ 9 5 2
♣ 10 6

3) How do you continue the auction with the North hands shown below after the following start to the auction?

SOUTH	NORTH
1♠	3♡
4♡	?

a) ♠ Q 9
♡ A K Q 7 4
♢ K Q 2
♣ 9 3 2

b) ♠ K Q 2
♡ A K J 10 4 3 2
♢ Q 3 2
♣ –

c) ♠ K Q 6
♡ K Q J 9 7 4
♢ K Q
♣ K 2

10. Pre-emptive Bidding

So far in our study of bidding we have been concerned solely with reaching our best contract. That is the proper objective when our side has the majority of the high cards, but when the position is reversed our objective must be to prevent the opponents making the best of their cards. Pre-emptive, or shut-out bids are not strong in high cards, but are based on long suits of seven or eight cards. The idea is to put up a barrage high enough to shut the opponents out of the auction, or at least make it risky for them to bid.

Often they will elect to double you rather than risk bidding at the four or five-level. It follows that you cannot afford to be too daring with your pre-emptive bids, or you may suffer an excessive penalty. To provide a reasonable margin of safety you should be within three tricks of your contract in your own hand if not vulnerable, and within two tricks if vulnerable.

Here are some examples:

(a) ♠ 7
     ♡ K Q J 10 8 6 3
     ◇ 10 7 3
     ♣ 8 4

(b) ♠ K Q J 9 7 4 3 2
     ♡ 6
     ◇ Q J 10
     ♣ 5

With hand (a) you expect to make six tricks with hearts as trumps. Open 3♡ if not vulnerable, but pass if vulnerable. Hand (b) is worth eight tricks in spades. Open 4♠ whether vulnerable or not.

Note that these are hands that are unsuitable for an opening one-level bid because of the lack of high cards.

Responding to Three-Bids

In his eagerness to shut out the opponents, partner may occasionally hit the wrong target, shutting you out instead. You should be able to picture partner's hand pretty accurately.

Generally you should play in his suit, and raise him only if you hold aces and kings. Suppose partner opens a non-vulnerable 3♡ and you hold these hands:

(c) ♠ K Q 8 3   (d) ♠ A 9 5 2
  ♡ 9   ♡ 9
  ♢ K Q 8 2   ♢ A K 8 5
  ♣ K Q J 9   ♣ A 9 4 3

Firstly hearts must be trumps. The idea that you should bid 3NT with (c) because 'he has the hearts and I have the other suits', is flawed because you need his hearts as a source of tricks. In no-trumps you will find great difficulty in gaining access to his hand if he has (a). Neither is raising to 4♡ sensible. If he has seven hearts he has only six cards in the other suits, and your queens will be useless opposite doubletons.

Hand (d) has a lower point count than (c), but is suitable for a raise to 4♡. Partner's six tricks, and your four make ten.

Quiz 8

1) What is your opening bid with these hands:
 i)   if not vulnerable?   ii)   if vulnerable?

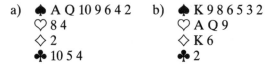

a) ♠ A Q 10 9 6 4 2   b) ♠ K 9 8 6 5 3 2
  ♡ 8 4   ♡ A Q 9
  ♢ 2   ♢ K 6
  ♣ 10 5 4   ♣ 2

2) How do you respond to your partner's vulnerable opening 3♡ with these hands?

a) ♠ A J 8 5 3 2   b) ♠ 8   c) ♠ A 9
  ♡ 6   ♡ A 8 4   ♡ 9 7 3
  ♢ A J 7   ♢ A Q 9 6 5 ♢ A 9 3 2
  ♣ A 10 2   ♣ 10 7 4 2   ♣ A K Q 2

11.   When Opponents Open

Half the time the bidding will be opened by your opponents. This does not mean that you have to keep silent, but you should understand the risk involved in entering the bidding when the opponent on your right has declared his strength. If you make an overcall on a flimsy suit you may find yourself sandwiched between two strong hands. Then the resulting penalty double will be heard two blocks away!

Before looking at specific hands it is sensible to consider how your priorities change when opponents open first.

Firstly, as we have seen, you are more likely to be doubled for penalties if you misjudge.

Secondly, the chances of your side having enough for game are reduced. It is more probable that you will end up contesting the part-score, as seen in the auction on page 13.

Thirdly, you must face the possibility that your side may lose the auction, and partner will have to make the opening lead. He will be inclined to lead your suit, so be wary of overcalling on a poor suit.

Consider your choices with these hands if your right-hand opponent opens 1♣ with neither side vulnerable.

(a)	♠ A 10 3	(b)	♠ K Q J 9 7 2
	♡ A 7 4		♡ 8 6 3
	◇ 9 6 2		◇ J 10 4
	♣ A J 7 3		♣ 6

You would certainly have opened (a) with 1NT, but to bid now would be asking for trouble. Firstly, you have no particular reason to want to be declarer. Your high cards are just as likely to take tricks in defence. Secondly, you have good reason to fear an enemy double, which could be costly. Hands that have opening bid values may not be worth an overcall. This is particularly true when your opponents have bid your suit.

Hand (b) illustrates the contrasting position. You would not have considered an opening bid with so few points. However your hand is probably worth five tricks if spades are trumps, as opposed to at most one if the opponents pick the trump suit. There is a great disparity between your *playing strength* and *defensive strength*, a sure sign that an overcall is worthy of consideration. There are two other points that point to a 1♠ intervention, known as an *overcall* of the enemy bid. Firstly, you want to suggest a spade lead if you lose the auction. Secondly, overcalling 1♣ with 1♠ stops the opponents bidding 1♡, and if they have a heart fit it may be hard for them to find it. The 1♠ overcall is surprisingly pre-emptive.

A one-level suit overcall shows about 9–16 points *and at least five cards in the overcalled suit*. A two-level overcall shows about 11–18 points, and usually a six-card suit.

Consider these hands if your right-hand opponent starts with 1◇ and nobody is vulnerable.

(c)   ♠ J 9 5 4 3   (d)   ♠ A Q J 8 5 4
      ♡ A Q   ♡ A 6
      ◇ K Q 2   ◇ 8 4
      ♣ 9 6 3   ♣ K Q 4

(e)   ♠ K Q J 9 7 6 2   (f)   ♠ A 10
      ♡ 8 6   ♡ A 7 4
      ◇ J 10 4   ◇ A J 10
      ♣ 6   ♣ K 10 4 3 2

Hand (c) is not suitable for a 1♠ overcall. The spades are too weak, making a double too likely. You should pass.

Hand (d) is too strong for 1♠. Make a *jump overcall* of 2♠, showing a good hand with a good 6-card or longer suit.

Note that just as in the uncontested auction it is a single jump that shows a strong hand. A double jump is our old friend the pre-emptive bid again. Bid 3♠ with hand (e).

Finally, you should overcall 1NT with (f). A 1NT overcall is the most dangerous of the lot as you don't have the security of a trump suit, so you need a balanced hand with 16–18 points and at least one guard in the enemy suit. It is risky, but so is passing as you might miss a game contract. Note that 1NT is better than 2♣ because the clubs are weak and you have two diamond stoppers.

Responding to Partner's Overcall

Since an overcall does not promise a great deal in the way of high card strength, you need not strain to keep the bidding open. Lacking support for partner's suit, you may pass with as many as 10 points. Raise freely when you have 3-card support, however. Remember, partner has at least five cards in his suit.

Suppose your left-hand opponent opens 1♡, partner overcalls 1♠ and the next player passes.

(g)	♠ 10 9 3 ♡ 8 7 6 4 ◇ A K J 5 ♣ 9 5	(h)	♠ Q 8 6 ♡ A 9 6 2 ◇ 4 ♣ K Q 7 6 3	(j)	♠ 9 7 6 2 ♡ 5 ◇ A K 8 5 ♣ A Q 6 4
	Raise to 2♠		Raise to 3♠		Raise to 4♠

The Take-out Double

With nobody vulnerable your right-hand opponent opens 1◇. What should you do with these hands?

(k)	♠ Q J 7 4 ♡ A Q 8 6 ◇ 2 ♣ K 10 6 2	(l)	♠ K Q 6 ♡ A J 9 3 ◇ 8 4 ♣ A 9 8 2	(m)	♠ A K 8 ♡ K J 5 2 ◇ 5 ♣ Q J 9 5 3

You want to compete against 1◇, but cannot pick a suit. Even with (m) where you have a 5-card club suit it is quite likely that partner will have sufficiently good spades or hearts to make a major suit contract preferable. Really you want partner to pick a suit. Do you have any ideas?

Consider how often you would use a penalty double here. Since partner could have nothing you would need a very strong hand and good trumps. Not very likely, is it? Even if you could punish 1♢ they may be able to escape successfully to 1♡ or 1♠. All in all, a penalty double of a suit contract is not very useful unless partner has shown strength. Therefore we abandon the use of a double for penalties and instead give the double a conventional meaning – *for takeout*.

Double with (k), (l) or (m) to show a three-suited overcall with opening values. However weak partner is he *must* pick one of the unbid suits and 'take out' the double, except in the rare instances when he has great strength in the enemy suit.

Of course it is very important to know when a double is for takeout. If partner has said anything other than 'no bid' your double will be interpreted as a penalty double, and will not be taken out. Equally a double of a no-trump bid, or of any bid at or above the four-level is for penalties.

Note that this means that double of an enemy three-level pre-emptive opening is for takeout. You need a little more than you would need for opening the bidding, maybe an ace more. You need all the gadgets you can muster to find your best contract after this devastating weapon is used against you.

Responding to a Take-out Double

Suppose 1♡ is opened on your left, partner doubles and the next player passes:

(n)	♠ 9 7 6 2	(p)	♠ K 10 4 3 2	(q)	♠ 4 3 2
	♡ 7 6 4		♡ 4 3		♡ K J 9 3
	♢ J 8 4 2		♢ 8 5 3		♢ Q 7 4
	♣ 6 3		♣ A 7 4		♣ 9 6 2

On a weak hand, such as (n) you bid your choice of suit as cheaply as possible, 1♠ [NF]. Hand (p) contains 8 points and a good major suit, and you must not make the same bid as on hand (n). Jump to 2♠ [NF] to indicate extra values.

Hand (q) is suitable for 1NT [NF], showing 6–10 HCP. As always when you choose no-trumps after an enemy bid you must have sound stoppers in their suit. Remember, partner's most likely heart holding is a singleton.

When the next player bids over your partner's double, you are relieved of the duty of finding a response on a weak hand. A voluntary response therefore shows some values, perhaps 5 or 6 points.

Counter to the Take-out Double

Let us change seats for a moment and consider the action that should be taken when partner's bid has been doubled for take-out.

If you have a good fit with partner you should remember the advice given on page 25, namely that you should bid aggressively with a good fit. Not only is it likely that you will make more tricks than you expect, but the better your fit the better fit your opponents are likely to have in their suit. It is normal to bid slightly higher than you would have done without the intervening double, hoping to pre-empt them out of the auction.

Suppose partner opens 1♠ and the next player doubles.

(r)	♠ Q 10 6 3 ♡ 5 2 ♢ Q 8 7 2 ♣ 9 7 5	(s)	♠ K Q 8 2 ♡ 5 2 ♢ Q J 10 5 ♣ 9 7 5	(t)	♠ Q J 8 3 2 ♡ 5 ♢ K 9 8 7 2 ♣ 10 5
	Raise to 2♠		Raise to 3♠		Raise to 4♠

You should not worry even if your contract drifts one off. It is an illusion to believe that you would have been left in peace to make your contract one level lower. Far more likely is that given extra bidding space the enemy would have got their act together and outbid you, making their contract.

Unless you have a good fit with partner it is usual for responder to ignore the intervening take-out double and bid naturally. However the double has made available an additional possibility to responder, and he should use it.

Suppose partner opens 1♠ and the next player doubles.

(u)   ♠ 8   (v)   ♠ 8 3
      ♡ A J 10 6   ♡ A J 10 6
      ◇ K Q 9 5   ◇ K Q 9 5 4
      ♣ K J 9 2   ♣ 9 2

With (u) you should be licking your lips in anticipation. Consider the evidence. You seem to have a misfit with your partner, which suggests the opponents' hands also fit badly. The misfit may be a handicap when it comes to declaring a contract, but it is good news in defence because your spade shortage lessens the possibility of partner's spade honours being trumped by declarer. Moreover your side has the majority of points. No doubt you can score game, but far more attractive and certain is the prospect of doubling them for penalties. The way to announce your intention to partner is to *redouble*.

The opposition double was for takeout so you don't expect to play in 1♠ redoubled, but if it happens you will shed no tears. You will make 1♠ redoubled by sheer brute strength, giving you game. More likely, however, the opponents will run from the redouble by bidding one of their suits, whereupon you will be delighted to double for penalties.

The redouble promises 10 or more points and denies 4-card support for partner. Redouble also with (v). You will be delighted to double either red suit, and will be content if partner can double a club contract.

Penalty Doubles

We have given up the possibility of doubling an enemy suit opening bid for penalties, in favour of the takeout double, but good prospects for penalty doubles still remain. Paradoxically, the most lucrative penalty doubles tend to occur at a low level. It is worth taking a little time to see why.

Suppose your opponents bid up to 4♡. Presumably they have taken several bids to get there, and each will have a good idea of his partner's assets. If things go badly for them you might beat them by a trick, but unless their bidding was foolish you won't get rich by doubling.

Contrast this with the position when an opponent overcalls, or makes a take-out double. He has to assume his partner has some assets, otherwise he will be cowed out of every auction. But if he is wrong, it will be your pleasure to make him pay. You have already seen how responder can threaten to penalise a take-out doubler with a redouble. Now consider hand (w) if partner opens 1♡ and the next player overcalls 1♠.

(w)	♠ A Q 9 7 6	(x)	♠ K 8	(y)	♠ K Q J 9 8
	♡ 9		♡ A 8 4		♡ K 8
	◇ K J 7 3		◇ K Q J 10 6		◇ 10 7 2
	♣ J 7 3		♣ K 5 2		♣ 10 5 3

You have got him! Your heart shortage is ideal for defending, and finding you with such excellent trumps will be most un-welcome news for declarer. Double for penalties. Note that this is a penalty double because partner has already bid.

The other type of low level penalty double is a double of no-trumps. If an opponent opens 1NT double on a hand with a good expectation of defeating the contract, for example hand (x). 16 points is normally the minimum requirement.

Finally, you don't need to give up completely on penalising an enemy opening suit bid. Suppose your right-hand opponent opens 1♠ and you hold (y). You may find it frustrating to pass, but just occasionally it will be your lucky day and partner will make a take-out double. He won't be too upset if you pass this and collect 500 or 800 above the line.

Defending Against their Pre-empt

You have seen how to pre-empt your opponents. Sadly they may also take pleasure in making life hard for you, so you need to consider your response to an enemy barrage. Suppose, with both sides vulnerable, your right-hand opponent opens 3♥. What do you do with these hands?

(a)	♠ K J 7 3	(b)	♠ K J 7	(c)	♠ 9 4
	♥ 8		♥ A Q 6		♥ K 9
	◇ A K 8 4		◇ A K 8 4		◇ A K Q J 6 3
	♣ A J 8 3		♣ J 10 2		♣ A 6 3

You need a positive attitude. The recommended bids are risky, and may result in a substantial penalty if partner is weak. A cowardly pass will just encourage them to make your life a misery every time they hold a weak hand with a long suit.

Hand (a) is a minimum takeout double of 3♥, about an ace stronger than a takeout double of 1♥.

With (b) bid 3NT, assuming (hoping) partner can help.

Also try 3NT with (c). You have a heart stopper, and plenty of tricks once you gain the lead.

Quiz 9

1) With the hands below what action do you take:
(i)   if your right-hand opponent opens 1♥?
(ii)   if your right-hand opponent opens 1♠?
(iii) if your right-hand opponent opens 1NT?

a)	♠ A Q J 7 3	b)	♠ 9	c)	♠ A J 8
	♥ 9 7 3		♥ A J 8 2		♥ K J 6
	◇ K 8		◇ K J 6 4 2		◇ Q J 7 2
	♣ 10 9 6		♣ A J 3		♣ Q 8 5

d)	♠ A J 8	e)	♠ A Q J 7 3 2	f)	♠ 9 6
	♥ K J 6		♥ 9 5		♥ K Q 6 2
	◇ A Q 7 2		◇ K 7 3		◇ A K 4
	♣ Q 8 5		♣ A Q		♣ Q 9 7 4

2) With the hands below what action do you take:
(i) if your left-hand opponent opens 1♡, partner overcalls 1♠ and your right-hand opponent passes?
(ii) if your left-hand opponent opens 1♡, partner doubles and right-hand opponent passes?
(iii) if your left-hand opponent opens 1♡, partner overcalls 1NT and right-hand opponent passes?

a) ♠ K J 7
    ♡ 9 6
    ◇ K 8 2
    ♣ A 8 6 4 3

b) ♠ K J 8 3 2
    ♡ 7
    ◇ K J 6
    ♣ 9 6 4 3

c) ♠ 8
    ♡ K Q 9 3 2
    ◇ K 7 4
    ♣ J 9 4 3

d) ♠ 9 7
    ♡ Q 7 4 3
    ◇ 10 8 5 2
    ♣ J 7 3

e) ♠ K 9 7 6 3 2
    ♡ 7
    ◇ 5 4
    ♣ 9 6 4 3

f) ♠ 8
    ♡ K Q J 10 9 6
    ◇ K 6 2
    ♣ 9 6 4

3) With the hands below what action do you take:
(i) if your partner opens 1♡ and the next hand doubles?
(ii) if your partner opens 1♠ and the next hand doubles?
(iii) if your partner opens 1♡ and the next hand overcalls 1♠?
(iv) if your partner opens 1♡ and the next hand overcalls 1NT?

a) ♠ K 10 9 6 3
    ♡ 9 8
    ◇ K J 10 6
    ♣ A 6

b) ♠ K Q 7 4 2
    ♡ 9 7
    ◇ J 9 7
    ♣ 9 5 2

c) ♠ A 9 5 2
    ♡ A 9 8 3
    ◇ 9 6
    ♣ 9 7 3

12. Developing Tricks at No-trumps

Chapters 12 and 13 explore the potential for taking tricks in a single suit. There are no trumps. The diagram for each shows the declarer holding and dummy. Try to play these combinations to make as many tricks as possible. Assume you can lead from either hand. You might find it helpful to construct the combinations from a pack, randomly dealing the missing cards to East and West.

Making Tricks by Brute Strength

Below are four card combinations that you might have to manipulate as declarer. They are unconnected (i.e., they are not the different suits of a single hand). In each case try to work out how many tricks you expect to take.

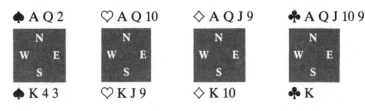

♠ A Q 2	♡ A Q 10	◇ A Q J 9	♣ A Q J 10 9
♠ K 4 3	♡ K J 9	◇ K 10	♣ K

The spade and heart holdings each provide three tricks. Despite having the top six hearts you cannot expect to take more than three heart tricks. To see why, try playing this combination. Suppose you start with the ♡A. The rules force you to play one of your 'winners' on the same trick. All your winners disappear on just three tricks.

In the minor suits there are the same cards as in hearts, but in diamonds you can make four tricks. Admittedly there will be wastage on the first two tricks, but dummy's last two diamonds will be able to take tricks separately. Note also that in playing diamonds it is correct to start with the ◇K, allowing you to take the second diamond trick in dummy and persevere with the suit. *Firstly cash the high cards from the shorter holding.*

In clubs there is even less wastage and you can make five tricks. Start with the ♣K and *overtake* it with dummy's ♣A, leaving you with the lead in the right hand to continue playing clubs. These tricks, being immediately cashable, are called *top tricks*.

To summarise:
In no-trumps the maximum number of tricks you can make in a suit is the number of cards held by the longer holding.

Now try to work out how many potential tricks you have with these holdings.

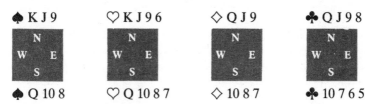

♠ K J 9   ♡ K J 9 6   ◇ Q J 9   ♣ Q J 9 8

♠ Q 10 8   ♡ Q 10 8 7   ◇ 10 8 7   ♣ 10 7 6 5

You have all of the top spades except the ace. This reduces the number of tricks by one, leaving you with two. Suppose you immediately play on spades. The defenders take their ♠A and lead another suit. You now have two spade tricks to cash. Similarly with hearts, once you have dislodged the ♡A you have three tricks for the taking.

In the minor suits you have two top cards missing, the ace and the king. If you need to score tricks you must patiently play on the suit, forcing out these missing honours, and regaining the lead in other suits. The diamonds then give you one trick and clubs provide two. *The maximum number of tricks you can make in a suit is the number of cards held by the longer holding, minus the number of top cards you must force out.*

It is worth mentioning now that it is natural for learners to have great fear of giving up the lead. We hope to calm your fears at the end of the chapter.

Who has the Missing Cards?

How many tricks do you expect to make with these combinations?

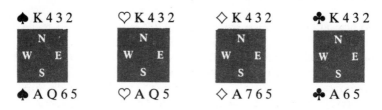

♠ K 4 3 2   ♡ K 4 3 2   ◇ K 4 3 2   ♣ K 4 3 2

♠ A Q 6 5   ♡ A Q 5   ◇ A 7 6 5   ♣ A 6 5

This time you cannot be sure. Consider the spade suit. There are five spades missing, the ♠ J 10 9 8 7. Suppose they are distributed as in diagram (a) below.

(a)   ♠ K 4 3 2   (b)   ♠ K 4 3 2

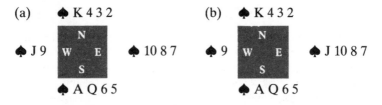

♠ J 9   ♠ 10 8 7   ♠ 9   ♠ J 10 8 7

♠ A Q 6 5   ♠ A Q 6 5

By the time you have cashed the ♠ A K Q neither opponent has a spade left. Nobody can beat your ♠6, which takes a fourth trick by *length*.

On the other hand they may be as in (b). This time your top three honours fail to draw the enemy spades and East's remaining ♠J prevents your ♠6 scoring.

There are two noteworthy points here.

Firstly, that while it does not require great skill to make tricks by brute strength, if you learn to take tricks with lowly sixes you are starting to master card skills.

Secondly, the trick-making capacity of your small cards may depend not only on which cards are missing, but also on who has them. You need a little bridge terminology here. In (a) one opponent has three spades and the other two. We say that the missing spades *break* 3–2. In (b) they break 4–1.

It is worth considering how to keep track of the enemy cards. Start by subtracting your 8 spades from 13. That leaves them with 5. Count them down as you play the suit. On the first round they both follow, so they now have 3, etc.

So how about the other suits on page 70?

You are missing six hearts and North's fourth heart will be worth a trick if hearts break 3–3.

The diamond suit will furnish a third trick if the missing five diamonds break 3–2. In that case cashing your $\diamond$ A K leaves just one enemy diamond at large, and you must force them to take it. Then the $\diamond$7 becomes a length winner.

Finally, if the clubs break 3–3 playing the ♣ A K and conceding a club will give you a third trick.

Losing the Lead in No-trumps

In many of our earlier examples we have shown how you can *establish* tricks, but only after you have given your opponents tricks in the suit. It is now time to examine these plays in the context of the whole hand.

Learners understandably have a fear of losing the lead, and must try to rationalise this fear. Consider the hands below.

(c)   ♠ A 3
     ♡ A Q 10
     ♢ A 9 6 4
     ♣ K J 10 9

(d)   ♠ A K 3
     ♡ A 7 4
     ♢ K 6 3
     ♣ K Q J 9

(c)   ♠ 9 6
     ♡ K J 9
     ♢ K Q J 10
     ♣ Q 8 7 6

(d)   ♠ 5 4 2
     ♡ K 8 6
     ♢ A 7 4
     ♣ 10 7 6 5

Contract: 3NT   *Lead:* ♠K   *Contract:* 3NT   *Lead:* ♠Q

In (c) you have the potential for making three club tricks after driving out the ace. You win the ♠A and continue with the ♣K, taken by West's ♣A. How many tricks do you expect to make now? Examine the suits one by one.

In spades you have just taken your only trick, the ♠A. You also have 3 heart tricks, 4 diamonds and 3 clubs.

That makes eleven, plenty for 3NT. Sadly there is a snag. Your opponents have the lead and they persevere with spades. Soon you are unable to follow suit in either hand. You are forced to discard your previous winners on the enemy spades.

Every learner suffers in this way, and the result is a natural desire to hang on grimly to the lead. The argument is: 'You can never tell what they will get up to if you give them the lead.'

It is important to realise that the deluge of spades that sank you was not black magic, and was not unpredictable. The problem was that you *lost control* of the spade suit. To play in a high-level no-trump contract you need sufficient strength in each suit to stop your opponents breaking through in that suit. Perhaps you were in the wrong contract. Perhaps you were a bit unlucky. After all if the enemy had led any other suit you would have wrapped up eleven tricks in comfort. There is often nothing you can do about such hands.

If you do have sufficient control in each suit you have nothing to fear from losing the lead. Consider hand (d).

Imagine initially that you make the error of cashing your top tricks, the ♠ A K, the ♡ A K and ◇ A K. What now?

One opponent now has two spade winners.

One opponent has two heart winners.

One opponent has two diamond winners.

You are still missing the ♣A and ♣K.

You can take the first six tricks, but that is your lot.

Now see what happens if you win the ♠A and turn your attention to clubs. An opponent takes the ♣A, but you have sufficient control of every suit to regain the lead. You end up taking nine tricks, the same six as before plus the three club tricks you have developed.

Do you see the difference?

At your first attempt you wrongly cashed the winners in your short suits. By doing so you set up winning tricks for enemy small honours and length cards.

Your second attempt was more successful because you kept the high cards in your short suits as *control cards*, and established tricks in *your* long suit.

Can you now see why it is usually sensible for each side to attack the suit where it has length rather than just high cards? The defender with the opening lead tries a long suit, hoping to drive out the enemy guards and eventually score length winners. Declarer pursues the same plan.

In hand (d) your red aces and kings cannot run away. They will take later tricks. The last trick taken counts for as much as the first.

If you don't have enough tricks for your contract you may have to give up the lead even when danger threatens. Suppose, playing 3NT, you have ♣ 9 8 5 3 in your hand and in dummy you have the singleton ♣A. Danger threatens when the enemy leads clubs. If you have enough immediate winners to fulfil your contract without relinquishing the lead it would be wise to take them quickly. But suppose you have just eight immediate winners, plus the ♡ K Q (although missing the ♡A). You must grit your teeth and lead a heart at trick 2.

If you are lucky the eight missing enemy clubs will break 4–4, allowing them to cash just three more club tricks. If clubs break 5–3 or worse you may be defeated, but *in this event there is nothing to be done*. Ensure your contract when it is possible to succeed, and do not worry about unavoidable failures.

Quiz 10

1) With each of the following suit combinations:
(i) Assuming you have plenty of leads to each hand and can afford to lose the lead a sufficient number of times, how many tricks do you hope to make?
(ii) Does your answer depend on the distribution of the missing cards? If so, then how?
(iii) If the suit behaves kindly for you, how many times do you expect to lose the lead before you can enjoy the fruits of your persistence?
(iv) State if the order of playing your honour cards matters.

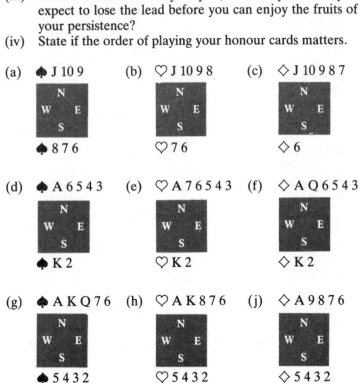

(a) ♠ J 10 9
     ♠ 8 7 6

(b) ♡ J 10 9 8
     ♡ 7 6

(c) ♢ J 10 9 8 7
     ♢ 6

(d) ♠ A 6 5 4 3
     ♠ K 2

(e) ♡ A 7 6 5 4 3
     ♡ K 2

(f) ♢ A Q 6 5 4 3
     ♢ K 2

(g) ♠ A K Q 7 6
     ♠ 5 4 3 2

(h) ♡ A K 8 7 6
     ♡ 5 4 3 2

(j) ♢ A 9 8 7 6
     ♢ 5 4 3 2

In the remaining four examples you are asked to consider setting up winners in the context of the whole hand.

2) ♠ Q J 4 3
♡ 5 3 2
♢ A K 4
♣ K 6 4

```
      N
  W       E
      S
```

♠ 10 9 6 5
♡ A K Q
♢ 5 3 2
♣ A 3 2

Contract: 3NT   *Lead:* ♡J

3) ♠ A 10 9
♡ 8 6 3
♢ Q 3
♣ 8 6 4 3 2

```
      N
  W       E
      S
```

♠ K Q J
♡ A K 7
♢ A K 2
♣ 10 9 7 5

Contract: 3NT   *Lead:* ♢J

4) ♠ A 5
♡ A Q J 10
♢ Q J 9 8
♣ K 9 3

```
      N
  W       E
      S
```

♠ 6 4 2
♡ K 9
♢ A K 10 7
♣ Q J 10 2

Contract: 3NT   *Lead:* ♠K

5) ♠ A 5
♡ A Q J
♢ Q J 9 8
♣ K 9 3 2

```
      N
  W       E
      S
```

♠ 6 4 2
♡ K 10 9
♢ A K 10 7
♣ Q J 10

Contract: 3NT   *Lead:* ♠K

13. The Finesse

You bid the following North/South hands to the correct contract of 7NT, and win the club lead in your hand with the ♣A. You are only missing three spades, the ♠ Q 10 and 9 and you start with the ♠A, but West gives your confidence a jolt by discarding a heart. Can you overcome this setback?

♠ 8 6 5 4 3
♡ K 10
♢ J 8 3
♣ 8 7 6

♠ A K J 7 2
♡ A 9
♢ A K Q
♣ A K Q

Well, at least you know where the missing spades are, so there is no temptation to bang down the ♠K, a play that would leave East with the winning ♠Q.

The winning play is to lead a spade from dummy, waiting to see with which card East follows before committing yourself to the ♠K or ♠J. Enter dummy at trick 3 with your invaluable ♡K and play the ♠4. If East follows with the ♠10 you win the trick with your ♠J, and the ♠K easily copes with his remaining ♠Q. Alternatively, if he makes the futile gesture of jumping in with the ♠Q you squash it with your ♠K and draw the ♠10 with your ♠J.

This play of leading from the weaker hand through a missing high card, towards the stronger hand is called a *finesse*.

In the previous example your finesse was bound to succeed, because you knew for certain that East had the missing ♠Q. Life usually isn't that easy. Try now to work out how many tricks you might expect to make with the spade holding below. You are allowed to lead from either hand, so you must presume that the other suits (not shown) provide you with the necessary entries.

♠ A Q 2

♠ 5 4 3

You certainly cannot expect to make any length tricks, because at least one opponent has four (or more) spades, so this time it is a question of trying to score tricks with honour cards that are not winners by force. We are really asking, how can you try to make a trick with the ♠Q? The two layouts below might give you some ideas.

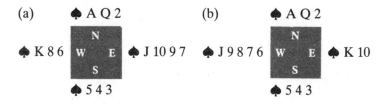

(a)   ♠ A Q 2   (b)   ♠ A Q 2

♠ K 8 6   W   E   ♠ J 10 9 7   ♠ J 9 8 7 6   W   E   ♠ K 10

♠ 5 4 3   ♠ 5 4 3

With (a) you can make a second spade trick, *provided you start by leading a low spade from the South hand*. The point is that West must then decide whether or not to play the ♠K before you commit yourself to dummy's card. If West plays his ♠K you head it with the ♠A and score the ♠Q by force. In the more likely event of West following with the ♠6 dummy's ♠Q can take the trick.

At this stage you may well protest. 'It is all very well saying that with all four hands on view, but how do I know that West has the ♠K when I can't see his hand?' You can't know. You assume West has the ♠K. If East has it, tough luck!

This is the most common finesse position, and it calls for a positive approach. Half the time West will have the ♠K and your ploy will be successful. The other half of the time East will have it and you will be unlucky. There is no point in agonising over this. If you require two spade tricks for your contract just be an optimist and go for it! That way you win some and lose some. Accept your fate calmly and you will conserve your energy for matters that you can influence.

Of course the layout could be as in diagram (b). Then playing the ♠A followed by the ♠2 will establish the ♠Q as a winner by force. So why take the finesse? You don't want a lecture in advanced mathematics, but it is a fact that while the finesse will work half of the time, a doubleton king will occur much less frequently. More often than not the missing spades will break 4–3, and even if they do break 5–2 it is more likely that the hand with five spades will also have the ♠K.

There is a crucial lesson here. It is possible that you might unsuccessfully take one line of play only to find that another (inferior) line would have worked. This happens to world champions! The best play doesn't always bring reward, but rest assured, in the long run you will gain far more than you lose by adopting the 'percentage' play. The world champion may lose one battle, but will invariably win the war.

A final thought on this combination. Just occasionally it might become clear that West cannot hold the ♠K. Maybe East opened 1NT (showing 12–14 points) and you have bought the contract in 4♡. By counting your points and dummy's you realise that you are only missing 14 points. That may be the time to play for layout (b).

If you are happy with that, what are your aspirations with the three suits below?

♡ A Q J   ◇ K 3 2   ♣ K Q 2

♡ 5 4 3   ◇ 6 5 4   ♣ 6 5 3

In hearts you can make *three* tricks if West has the ♡K. Following the general principle of leading from the weaker hand towards the stronger hand, you start with South's ♡3. If West plays low, try dummy's ♡J. If it wins return to the South hand with another suit and try again. West, holding the ♡K, must each time sit there impotently.

In diamonds you can make dummy's ◇K if West has the ◇A. Start with the ◇4 from South and make West commit himself.

In clubs you can make two tricks if West has the ♣A. Start with the ♣3. West plays low and dummy's ♣K wins. Return to your hand with another suit and continue with the ♣ 5. West is helpless.

The following combinations illustrate the same principle but are somewhat more difficult.

♠ A Q 10   ♡ K J 5   ◇ K 10 5

♠ 4 3 2   ♡ 4 3 2   ◇ 4 3 2

In the spade suit there are two crucial missing cards, the ♠K and ♠J. There are four possible positions for these cards, as shown below:

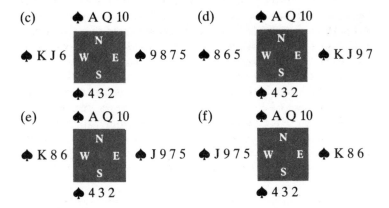

Assuming your objective is to make as many tricks as possible, try to be a super-optimist, and hope for West to hold the ♠K and ♠J, as in layout (c). Lead the ♠2 from South's hand, and cover whichever card West plays. Normally West will contribute the ♠6, and this allows dummy's ♠10 to take a cheap trick. Return to the South hand by using another suit and repeat the torture, this time scoring with the ♠Q.

Of course however optimistic you are the cards reserve the right to kick you in the teeth. In layout (d) dummy's ♠10 will lose to East's ♠J. Later you might try finessing dummy's ♠Q only to suffer a similar fate as East produces the ♠K. Such is life!

Diagrams (e) and (f) illustrate the 'in-between' positions. In (e) the ♠10 will lose to the ♠J, but a later finesse of the ♠Q will reward your persistence. In (f), to beat the ♠10 East must part with his ♠K, leaving you with two winners in dummy. Win some, lose some!

So how about the hearts? Again the super-optimist will lead from South and try dummy's ♡J if West plays low. With the aid of a subsequent finesse of the ♡K two tricks are available if West has the ♡A and ♡Q. No trick will be made, however, if East has both missing honours.

Finally, how about diamonds? Armed with your increasing experience you will no doubt be raring to lead from the South hand intending to finesse dummy's ♦K. But wait a minute. Why not try dummy's ♦10? Just occasionally West will have been dealt the ♦Q and ♦J, so the ♦10 will force East to waste the ♦A on the trick.

Does that sound unlikely? Well, perhaps it is, but the fact is that if losing the lead is not a problem, this is a chance to nothing. If the ♦10 loses to the ♦Q or ♦J you can always revert to your original plan and finesse the ♦K later.

Note that once again the question rears its head of how inconvenient will it be to lose the lead. The point is that while you can consider the play of a suit in isolation, in real life that suit is surrounded by three others, each of which might offer an opportunity or conceal a hidden danger. You first learn the *techniques* for generating extra tricks. You then acquire the overall vision and *judgement* necessary to determine when each technique is appropriate.

Real and Imaginary Finesses

As usual you are being asked to play the suit combinations below to generate as many tricks as possible.

♠ A 3 2 ♡ A 3 2 ♦ A 3 2

♠ Q J 10 ♡ J 10 9 ♦ Q 5 4

In spades you should enter the South hand by means of another suit and lead the ♠Q. You are hoping that West has the ♠K, so if West fails to play it you *don't* change your mind and play dummy's ♠A. Will it help West to cover the ♠Q with the ♠K? In this case the answer is 'No', *because you possess the ♠J and ♠10*. West's ♠K would seemingly take a noble sacrificial role in taking out your ♠Q and ♠A, but the cards *promoted* to winning status belong to you.

The heart suit will provide two tricks if West has either the ♡Q or ♡K. As South you play the ♡J, and allow it to run to East if West fails to cover. Suppose East takes the trick with the ♡K and you regain the lead on the next trick. You can now finesse similarly against West's presumed ♡Q.

The diamond suit illustrates the type of situation which learners find hard to recognise. They realise that if West has the ◇K they can prevent this card from taking a trick by leading the ◇Q from South, waiting for West's reaction. Sadly this doesn't help. Consider layout (g), which presumably is what is hoped for.

(g) ◇ A 3 2   (h)   ◇ A 3 2

◇ K 8 6   N / W E / S   ◇ J 10 9 7   ◇ J 10 9 7   N / W E / S   ◇ K 8 6

◇ Q 5 4   ◇ Q 5 4

West foils the plan by covering the ◇Q with the ◇K. Dummy's ◇A takes the trick, but there are no further tricks for declarer *because East has the remaining top diamonds*. This is the purpose behind the defensive maxim 'Cover an honour with an honour.' Leading an honour, hoping to smoke out an enemy honour, is pointless if all you are doing is promoting tricks for your opponents.

In fact, the diamond layout you should be hoping for is (h). You can make two diamond tricks if *East* has the ◇K. Start by cashing dummy's ◇A, and follow up with a small diamond from the North hand, forcing East to make a commitment.

Quiz 11

1) With each of the following suit combinations:

(i) Assuming you can afford to lose the lead a sufficient number of times and you have ample entries to either hand, how many tricks do you hope to make?

(ii) How does the success of your plan depend on the position of the missing cards?

(iii) How do you intend to play the suit?

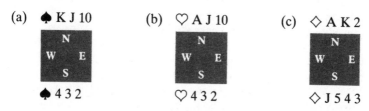

(a) ♠ K J 10

♠ 4 3 2

(b) ♡ A J 10

♡ 4 3 2

(c) ◇ A K 2

◇ J 5 4 3

In the remaining two examples you are asked to consider setting up winners in the context of the whole hand.

2) ♠ A 5
♡ 9 6 4 2
◇ 8 4 2
♣ K Q J 2

♠ 7 4 3
♡ A Q 3
◇ A K 6
♣ A 10 4 3

i) *Contract:* 2NT *Lead:* ♠K
ii) *Contract:* 3NT *Lead:* ♠K

3) ♠ A K Q
♡ A K Q
◇ K Q 2
♣ A 6 5 2

♠ 5 4 3
♡ 5 3 2
◇ A 4 3
♣ Q J 4 3

Contract: 6NT *Lead:* ◇J

14.   Using a Trump Suit

The suit combinations you have met so far are not affected by the presence or otherwise of a trump suit. So why have a trump suit, bearing in mind that no-trump contracts score better? The reasons for choosing a suit contract can be divided into two main categories.

Using Trumps for Control

In previous chapters you have met examples where your ability to play a suit to your best advantage depended on how well you controlled other suits. Playing in no-trumps, it can be most frustrating to lose the lead while establishing winners only to find that you cannot regain it because opponents cash their winners. The first purpose of a trump suit is to swing the balance of control in your favour. Consider these hands.

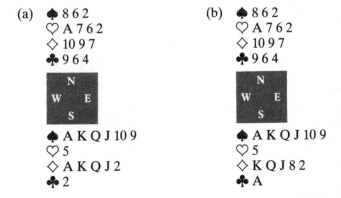

(a)   ♠ 8 6 2
      ♡ A 7 6 2
      ◇ 10 9 7
      ♣ 9 6 4

      N
      W   E
      S

      ♠ A K Q J 10 9
      ♡ 5
      ◇ A K Q J 2
      ♣ 2

(b)   ♠ 8 6 2
      ♡ A 7 6 2
      ◇ 10 9 7
      ♣ 9 6 4

      N
      W   E
      S

      ♠ A K Q J 10 9
      ♡ 5
      ◇ K Q J 8 2
      ♣ A

Imagine playing (a) in no-trumps. West leads the ♣A and continues clubs. Despite having twelve winners you have to discard a number of them on West's clubs. In the best scenario the missing clubs will break 5–4, but there will be only eight tricks left by the time you gain the lead.

Now try playing the same layout with spades as trumps. You lose trick 1 to the ♣A, but can trump the ♣K continuation. Having played high trumps until the enemy have none left (known as drawing trumps) you then start on diamonds. This time you make twelve tricks, a small slam.

Playing (b) in no-trumps you seem to be better off with a control card in each suit, but that is an illusion. You can indeed grasp trick 1 with the ♣A, but you can take only eight tricks before you have to turn your attention to diamonds. Your opponents will then take the rest. Your one club control was insufficient, being knocked out before you could realise your assets.

Playing in spades is again much better. You draw the enemy trumps, drive out the ◇A, trump the ♣K continuation and make twelve tricks.

This theme is typical of suit play. You should pick a trump suit in which you have at least eight cards, leaving the defenders with at most five. Play sufficient trumps to leave you with some, but them with none. You can then trump their side suit winners, but they cannot retaliate.

Now try your skill at (c) and (d).

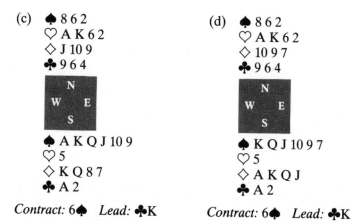

(c) ♠ 8 6 2
     ♡ A K 6 2
     ◇ J 10 9
     ♣ 9 6 4

     ♠ A K Q J 10 9
     ♡ 5
     ◇ K Q 8 7
     ♣ A 2

Contract: 6♠ Lead: ♣K

(d) ♠ 8 6 2
     ♡ A K 6 2
     ◇ 10 9 7
     ♣ 9 6 4

     ♠ K Q J 10 9 7
     ♡ 5
     ◇ A K Q J
     ♣ A 2

Contract: 6♠ Lead: ♣K

In (c) you take your ♣A and draw trumps. Did you then try to drive out the ◇A? Too bad! They cash a club trick to defeat you. You must cash the ♡ A K (throwing the ♣2) before touching diamonds. Then when West takes the ◇A you can trump a club continuation and safeguard your twelve tricks.

This is straightforward once you recognise the danger, but how could you anticipate it? The secret lies in counting your *losers*. Your hand will lose the ◇A and one club, unless you can find a winning card in dummy which you can use to discard a club. That card is the ♡K. If West hadn't led a club there would be no urgency as you would still have the ♣A as protection. However, the club lead has left you with a problem that requires immediate solution. Recognising the problem puts you half way to solving it!

How about (d)? Again you have the urgent problem of two losers (the ♠A and a club), and again the solution is to pair up dummy's ♡K with your ♣2. This time you cannot even afford the luxury of drawing trumps before you dispose of your losing club because to do so would involve losing the lead. Take your ♣A and immediately cash the ♡ A K.

To summarise:
When you play in a trump contract it is usually correct to play on trumps until the defenders have none left. The purpose of this is to allow you to cash your side suit winners in peace, without fear of losing them to an enemy ruff. However sometimes there are reasons not to draw trumps, for example, the need to eliminate losers first.

Cross-ruffing

How many spade tricks do you expect to make if you have the top twelve spades, six in each hand:
(i)   in no-trumps?   (ii)   with spades as trumps?
(i)   When playing in no-trumps you are limited to six spade tricks, because neither hand has more than six spades.
(ii)   If spades are trumps consider these layouts. In (e) West leads the ♣K to your ♣A. What next?

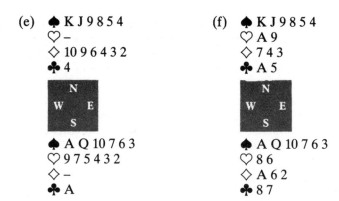

(e) ♠ K J 9 8 5 4
♡ –
♢ 10 9 6 4 3 2
♣ 4

♠ A Q 10 7 6 3
♡ 9 7 5 4 3 2
♢ –
♣ A

(f) ♠ K J 9 8 5 4
♡ A 9
♢ 7 4 3
♣ A 5

♠ A Q 10 7 6 3
♡ 8 6
♢ A 6 2
♣ 8 7

Earlier you were advised to draw the enemy trumps unless you have good reason to do otherwise. In this section you will see a number of hands where you do have reason to either delay drawing trumps, or even to abandon it completely.

Here you want to make all your trumps separately by alternately trumping hearts in dummy and diamonds in your hand. This process is called a *cross-ruff*. In this case you are guaranteed success because all your trumps are higher than any of those possessed by the defenders. At the end East or West is subject to the indignity of under-ruffing, i.e., discarding the ♠2 under your high trump. Despite the fact that you have just fourteen HCP you make all thirteen tricks.

Sadly, playing in a trump suit doesn't necessarily guarantee that you can make your trumps separately in this manner. Playing (f) in a spade contract, you can never make more than six spade tricks because the other suits have mirror-image shape between the North and South hands. You might as well play in 3NT.

Of course most hands fall in between these two extremes. It is common to be able to make one or two extra tricks by playing in a suit contract, hence it is normal to prefer a contract of 4♠ to 3NT if you have a eight-card or better spade fit.

When cross-ruffing it is easy to overlook one potential danger. What do you think your opponents will be doing while you are cross-ruffing? They will be discarding cards in other suits. If you complete your cross-ruff and *then* try to cash your side suit winners, you will be sadly disappointed because somebody will ruff.

Try playing (e) again if the lead is the ♡A. If you cross-ruff the first twelve tricks, at trick 13 one of your opponents will ruff the ♣A with the ♠2. You must cash your ♣A first.

Before cross-ruffing cash your winners in the side suits.

Ruffing Losers in Dummy

Look at (g) and (h). Nine tricks are easy. Can you find a tenth?

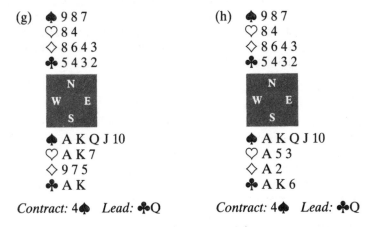

(g)
```
    ♠ 9 8 7
    ♡ 8 4
    ◇ 8 6 4 3
    ♣ 5 4 3 2

    ♠ A K Q J 10
    ♡ A K 7
    ◇ 9 7 5
    ♣ A K
```
Contract: 4♠ *Lead:* ♣Q

(h)
```
    ♠ 9 8 7
    ♡ 8 4
    ◇ 8 6 4 3
    ♣ 5 4 3 2

    ♠ A K Q J 10
    ♡ A 5 3
    ◇ A 2
    ♣ A K 6
```
Contract: 4♠ *Lead:* ♣Q

With (g) you seem to have four losers in your hand: one heart and three diamonds. The key to finding your extra trick lies in the fact that dummy has one heart fewer than your hand. Having won the ♣A you must postpone drawing trumps. At tricks 2 and 3 cash the ♡ A K then ruff the ♡7.

Note that the source of the extra trick is the act of ruffing a loser in the hand with the *shorter* trumps. Your original count of five trump winners was based on the five spades in your hand, the hand with the longer trumps. It is tempting to regard the trumping of any loser as the gain of a trick, but ruffing in the hand with longer trumps gives you a trick that you were going to take anyway. Indeed, shortening your longer trump holding can seriously damage your prospects by causing you to lose control.

With (h) you also need to trump a heart in dummy, but this time you need to prepare your ground. Win the ♣A, cash the ♡A and give up a heart trick. Of course there is an element of danger in this as your ♣K could then be ruffed, but you have no choice. Assuming you safely regain the lead at trick 4 you can ruff your ♡5 in dummy, before drawing trumps.

Ruffing losers in dummy has the same objective as cross-ruffing, namely, making extra tricks from your trump suit, but the techniques are different. When cross-ruffing you cash all your side suit winners first, accepting that you don't intend to draw trumps. When ruffing losers in dummy you normally aim to retain control, eventually drawing trumps and then cashing your other side suit winners in safety.

Using Trumps to Help Establish a Side Suit

You are handling the combinations shown below in a no-trump contract, with plenty of entries to either hand. Assuming that it is safe to lose the lead as often as is necessary:

(i) How many tricks do you hope to make?

(ii) How many times do you expect to lose the lead in order to fulfil your expectation?

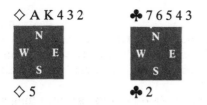

♢ A K 4 3 2   ♣ 7 6 5 4 3

♢ 5   ♣ 2

You must hope that the missing diamonds break 4–3. In that case you can cash the ◇ A K, concede two diamonds to the defenders and subsequently make a length trick. You will make three tricks, losing the lead twice.

In clubs it will probably hardly occur to you that it is possible to make any tricks, indeed you are far more likely to be apprehensive as to how many club tricks your opponents will take. Nevertheless if the missing clubs break 4–3, it will be possible for you to make one length trick after losing the lead four times.

How about the same suits played in a suit contract?

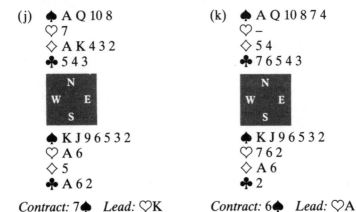

(j) ♠ A Q 10 8
    ♡ 7
    ◇ A K 4 3 2
    ♣ 5 4 3

    ♠ K J 9 6 5 3 2
    ♡ A 6
    ◇ 5
    ♣ A 6 2

Contract: 7♠ Lead: ♡K

(k) ♠ A Q 10 8 7 4
    ♡ –
    ◇ 5 4
    ♣ 7 6 5 4 3

    ♠ K J 9 6 5 3 2
    ♡ 7 6 2
    ◇ A 6
    ♣ 2

Contract: 6♠ Lead: ♡A

What are you going to do about your club losers in (j)? One can be discarded on the ◇K and for the other you must establish a diamond length trick. Played in spades you can generate exactly the same number of club winners as you could in no-trumps, but you needn't lose any tricks.

Win the ♡A and draw trumps with the ♠ A Q. Now cash the ◇ A K (pitching the ♣2) and ruff the ◇2. If both opponents follow suit you know that the enemy diamonds are breaking 4–3, so you are home and dry. Cross to dummy by trumping the ♡6 and ruff the ◇3. Finally re-enter dummy with a trump and triumphantly throw your ♣6 on the master ◇4. If you have difficulty following this sequence construct the hands from a pack of cards, giving West four diamonds and East three, and distribute the other cards randomly.

Before leaving this example it is important that you are clear about the source of your extra trick. It did not come from ruffing the diamonds in your hand. Admittedly you did win these tricks with tiny trumps, but you were always going to make these trumps simply by playing out trumps from the top. Ruffing in the hand with long trumps only generates extra tricks if you do it so often that the other hand ends up with more trumps, a technique called a *dummy reversal* which is beyond the scope of this book. The extra trick materialised because your ruffing manoeuvre established a length trick in dummy.

Playing (k) again you can establish a length trick, this time in clubs, provided the missing clubs break 4–3. Ruff the ♡A, and concede a club trick. Win the return and you can repeatedly re-enter dummy (by ruffing hearts and using trumps as entries) and ruff clubs until the ♣7 is a winner. You were lucky that West didn't lead a diamond!

Quiz 12

1) ♠ J 5 4 3 2
   ♡ 6 2
   ◇ 8 7 6
   ♣ Q 8 7

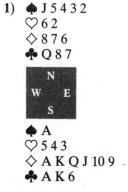

   ♠ A
   ♡ 5 4 3
   ◇ A K Q J 10 9
   ♣ A K 6

Contract: 5◇ *Lead:* ♠K

2) ♠ A 4 3 2
   ♡ K 10 8 7
   ◇ 9 8 3 2
   ♣ 5

   ♠ 8
   ♡ A Q J 9
   ◇ A 6 5 4
   ♣ A 8 7 6

Contract: 4♡ *Lead:* ◇K

3) ♠ A K Q
♡ 4 2
◇ 10 5
♣ A K 8 5 3 2

♠ J 10 9 8 7 6
♡ A 3
◇ A 8 2
♣ 7 6

Contract: 7♠ *Lead:* ◇K
Trumps break 2–2.
If you feel inspired you might
like to consider what to do if
trumps break 3–1.

4) ♠ 10 6 5
♡ A K 4
◇ K 6 4 2
♣ J 4 3

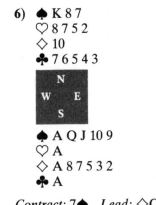

♠ K Q J 9 8 7
♡ 5 3 2
◇ Q
♣ K Q 10

Contract: 4♠ *Lead:* ♡Q

5) ♠ 5 3 2
♡ A 7 6 4 3
◇ Q 4 3
♣ A 2

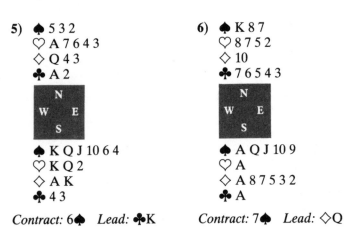

♠ K Q J 10 6 4
♡ K Q 2
◇ A K
♣ 4 3

Contract: 6♠ *Lead:* ♣K

6) ♠ K 8 7
♡ 8 7 5 2
◇ 10
♣ 7 6 5 4 3

♠ A Q J 10 9
♡ A
◇ A 8 7 5 3 2
♣ A

Contract: 7♠ *Lead:* ◇Q

15. Entries and Communications

You have already started to estimate how many winners you have available in each suit, and how many losers a hand has. Your ability to develop and use winners depends on a number of factors, for example whether your losers will catch up with you before you can enjoy your winners. Another crucial matter is whether you have enough entries to accomplish your goal.

When taking finesses in chapter 13 we allowed you to assume as many entries as you needed to either hand. In real life the most attractive line of play can be rendered impractical by lack of entries. You must learn to recognise such situations and look for another, more realistic line. On other occasions the entries will be present as long as you nurture them.

Neither of the hands below may seem a problem, but carelessness could prove costly.

(a) ♠ A 5 4 3
    ♡ 5 4 3
    ♢ A 4 3
    ♣ 6 3 2

```
      N
   W     E
      S
```

    ♠ K Q
    ♡ A K Q J 10
    ♢ K 5 2
    ♣ A K Q

Contract: 7NT   *Lead:* ♢Q

(b) ♠ A K Q J
    ♡ A 3 2
    ♢ A K Q 2
    ♣ K Q

```
      N
   W     E
      S
```

    ♠ 6 3 2
    ♡ J 10 6
    ♢ 9 6
    ♣ A J 10 3 2

Contract: 7NT   *Lead:* ♠4

In (a) you have thirteen winners (3 spades, 5 hearts, the $\diamond$ A K and 3 clubs). Your hand seems to have a diamond loser (not two as one diamond is covered by dummy's $\diamond$A), but you have dummy's ♠A for a discard. So what can go wrong?

The danger lies in the *blocked* spade suit. Whenever you have honours in a suit without accompanying small cards to provide access to honours in the opposite hand, beware! You will be all right provided you can cash your ♠ K Q, and then enter dummy in another suit in order to take the ♠A. The necessary entry to dummy is the $\diamond$A, so don't squander it at trick 1. It is imperative to win the opening lead with your $\diamond$K.

How about (b)? The club suit is blocked, and this time there is no side suit entry to the South hand. You must cash the ♣K and overtake the ♣Q with your ♣A. As long as the clubs break 3–3 or 4–2 you will be able to score a fifth club trick with the ♣3. If they are 5–1 you will, no doubt, feel foolish squandering the ♣A on the ♣Q and then failing to make a fifth club, but there was nothing you could have done about it.

Now try (c) and (d). Be reassured that we have not taken leave of our senses. The hands are *not* the same.

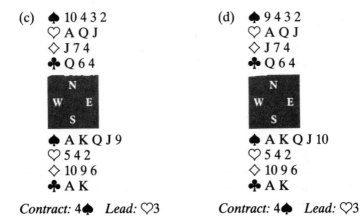

(c)   ♠ 10 4 3 2
      ♡ A Q J
      $\diamond$ J 7 4
      ♣ Q 6 4

      ♠ A K Q J 9
      ♡ 5 4 2
      $\diamond$ 10 9 6
      ♣ A K

Contract: 4♠   *Lead:* ♡3

(d)   ♠ 9 4 3 2
      ♡ A Q J
      $\diamond$ J 7 4
      ♣ Q 6 4

      ♠ A K Q J 10
      ♡ 5 4 2
      $\diamond$ 10 9 6
      ♣ A K

Contract: 4♠   *Lead:* ♡3

Start by considering the similarities between the two hands. In each case you have three losing diamonds in each hand and a possible fourth loser if East has the ♡K. Also, in each case you have a surplus club winner in dummy, the ♣Q. If this can be used to discard a losing diamond your problems are over, since even if you lose a heart trick, two diamond losers and one heart loser will not sink 4♠. It will not help you much to discard a heart loser as you could still lose three diamonds and a heart.

The question now is whether or not you take the heart finesse at trick 1. If you do so and it fails, it is highly likely that the defenders will cash three diamond tricks, leaving you with nothing to discard on dummy's ♣Q. So how about giving up on the heart finesse, rising with the ♡A and aiming to draw trumps, throwing a diamond away on the ♣Q? Before deciding, you must check that communications between the two hands make your plan feasible.

In diagram (c) you can take the ♡A, cash the ♠ A K Q and the ♣ A K, and enter dummy by overtaking the ♠9 with the ♠10. Now throw the ◇6 on the ♣Q and drive out the ♡K, losing just two diamonds and the ♡K.

Can you see the different in (d)? This time there is no ♠10 in dummy, so you cannot easily reach your ♣Q. There is no point in playing to the first six tricks as in (a) and spotting the problem only when it is too late. Your only realistic chance is to take the heart finesse at trick 1. If successful you will make eleven tricks, otherwise a diamond switch will hold you to nine. The idea is to do all your thinking at trick 1, resulting in a plan which will succeed if the crucial cards (in this case the ♡K) lie kindly.

Holding up a winner

When the opponents attack in their long suit there may be an advantage in refusing to take your winner in the suit immediately. If you play low, making no attempt to take the trick when you could have done so, that is called 'holding up' your winner.

Learners can find this concept hard to swallow. It is bad enough to have to take a finesse, where at least you are trying to generate an extra trick. What if your ace never scores a trick?

Such fears are entirely understandable, but it is when you can be gently coaxed away from them that the path to expertise begins to open up. It is very rare for an ace to vanish into thin air, and there are far more important considerations.

In each of the diagrams below consider how many tricks the defenders (East/West) can hope to make against 3NT in the suit shown. They lead the suit at trick 1, and South has to concede a trick early to the ♠A.

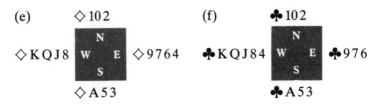

This is the same type of question as you faced in chapter 12, but then you were declarer. The answer seems to be that East/West can make three diamonds and four clubs, but look closely at the club position. Suppose West leads the suit but declarer holds up his ♣A on the first and second round of the suit, taking the ♣A on the third round. Unless he has the ♠A as an entry card West cannot gain the lead to cash the winning clubs. If East has the ♠A, East will have no club to return.

Holding up a stopper is a play designed to sabotage the enemy lines of communication, as in the example above.

The Duck

A similar play of a low card from both hands where declarer could have won the trick is called a 'duck'. In this case the purpose is constructive rather than obstructive. The declarer ducks in order to facilitate his own communications.

The difference between the duck and the hold-up is shown in (g) and (h).

(g)
- ♠ 7 6 4
- ♡ 6 5 3
- ♢ A 7 4 3 2
- ♣ 7 6

```
    N
W       E
    S
```

- ♠ A K
- ♡ A 8 4 2
- ♢ K 6 5
- ♣ A K 5 4

Contract: 3NT *Lead:* ♠Q

(h)
- ♠ 4 2
- ♡ 6 5
- ♢ A Q J 10 9
- ♣ K 8 4 3

```
    N
W       E
    S
```

- ♠ A 5 3
- ♡ A K J 4
- ♢ 8 6 2
- ♣ A 6 2

Contract: 3NT *Lead:* ♠Q

With (g) you have seven top tricks and it will be possible to develop two length tricks in diamonds if they break 3–2. If you cash your ♢ A K and then concede a diamond you will have no entry to dummy and your two established diamonds will be unusable. Instead you must win the ♠ A, cash your ♢K and *then* duck a diamond. Now the ♢A will provide the crucial entry to dummy *at the right moment*. The purpose of ducking the second diamond trick is to *preserve your communications*, and ensure access to dummy's winners.

With (h) you must hold up your ♠A twice if the suit is led. Now if the diamond finesse fails East may have no spade to return. The purpose of playing low twice in spades is to *disrupt the enemy communications*, and prevent them from cashing their winners.

Finally, a word of advice. Only decline a trick if you have a precise purpose in mind. In particular, don't hold up a trick in a suit led by your opponents if there is the danger that they will find an even more harmful switch to another suit.

Quiz 13

1) ♠ 5 2
♡ K J 7
◇ 7 6 5 4
♣ 7 6 3 2

♠ A Q J 10 9 8
♡ A Q 10
◇ A K
♣ A 8

Contract: 6♠ *Lead:* ♣K

2) ♠ A J 9 5 2
♡ A 6 5
◇ 7
♣ A 7 6 3

♠ 7 6
♡ K 4
◇ A K Q 5 4 3
♣ 8 5 4

Contract: 3NT *Lead:* ♡Q

3) ♠ A 5 3 2
♡ Q J 8 4
◇ K Q
♣ 9 6 2

♠ 7 6 4
♡ A K
◇ A 6 3 2
♣ A 8 4 3

i) *Contract:* 3NT *Lead:* ♠K
ii) *Contract:* 3NT *Lead:* ♣K

4) ♠ 4
♡ A 3 2
◇ 7 6 5 4
♣ K J 10 3 2

♠ A K Q J 10
♡ K 5 4
◇ A K Q 8
♣ Q

Contract: 6NT *Lead:* ♡J

5) ♠ A K Q
♡ 7 6
◇ K 5 4 3 2
♣ 10 5 2

♠ 7 4 3
♡ A 8 2
◇ Q J 10 9
♣ A K Q

Contract: 3NT   *Lead:* ♡Q

6) ♠ 5 4
♡ 6 3 2
◇ 9 4
♣ A K 8 7 5 2

♠ A K 7 3
♡ A 5 4
◇ A J 3 2
♣ 4 3

Contract: 3NT   *Lead:* ♠Q

7) ♠ 3 2
♡ A 5 3
◇ 8 7 6 3
♣ K Q 10 9

♠ A 10
♡ 9 2
◇ K Q J 10 9
♣ A J 8 7

Contract: 3NT   *Lead:* ♡K

8) ♠ A K
♡ 9 8 5 2
◇ A Q 5
♣ A K Q J

♠ Q 4 3 2
♡ A 7 6
◇ 6 3 2
♣ 8 7 4

Contract: 3NT   *Lead:* ◇4

16. Winners and Losers

Some of the hands you have already seen show clearly the need
for careful planning. Indeed, the most crucial and wide ranging
general piece of advice we can give is *to form a plan before you
play a single card.* There are a number of things you need to focus
on: Losers, immediate winners (or top tricks), winners that can
definitely be developed, and possible extra tricks (e.g., by a
finesse).

Try your skill at the examples below.

(a) ♠ K Q 4 2　　　　(b) ♠ Q 4 3
　　 ♡ A 5　　　　　　　　 ♡ K 9 4 2
　　 ♢ 8 5 4 3　　　　　　 ♢ J 8
　　 ♣ 9 5 4　　　　　　　 ♣ Q 5 3 2

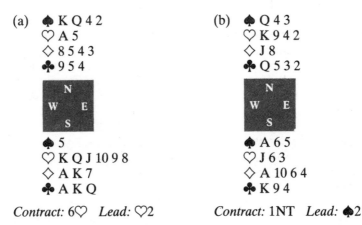

　　 ♠ 5　　　　　　　　　 ♠ A 6 5
　　 ♡ K Q J 10 9 8　　　　 ♡ J 6 3
　　 ♢ A K 7　　　　　　　 ♢ A 10 6 4
　　 ♣ A K Q　　　　　　　 ♣ K 9 4

Contract: 6♡　*Lead:* ♡2　　　*Contract:* 1NT　*Lead:* ♠2

We try to summarise the question-and-answer thought process
that you should go through for (a).

Q 'How many winners have I got?'
A '12. One spade, 6 hearts, 2 diamonds, 3 clubs.'
Q 'How many immediate losers?'
A 'Just one, the ♠A'
Q 'This seems a highly satisfactory state of affairs. Can I
　 anticipate any avoidable problems?'

This is the difficult bit because it depends on recognition. If you
automatically draw trumps you will find that you have no entry to

dummy's established spade, and in the fullness of time you will find yourself with a diamond loser.

So how can you learn to recognise such a problem without an infinite amount of time at your disposal? Asking yourself an endless barrage of questions, e.g., 'Are there entry problems?', will not only exhaust you but drive everybody else mad! We think the solution is similar to learning a foreign language. You cannot conduct a conversation by looking up every word in a dictionary or constantly reciting irregular verbs. To learn you must practice until it comes intuitively.

In the meantime when dummy goes down, hold your cards in one hand and sit on the other. This prevents you from grabbing a card before you have considered your strategy.

Now we return to example (a). You recognise that you have an entry problem for dummy's spades, and the only entry to dummy is the ♡A. Therefore win the opening lead *in your hand*, and lead a spade at trick 2. Suppose East takes the ♠K with the ♠A and returns a diamond. Take it with the ♢A, enter dummy with the ♡A, and discard your diamond loser on the established ♠Q. Then ruff a spade back to your hand and complete the drawing of trumps.

Note that good planning has led you to ignore two guidelines. You haven't immediately drawn trumps, and you blocked the heart suit by failing to take the ♡A on the first round.

How about (b)? We have been mischievous here. It isn't remotely possible to plan this. Indeed, when you gain the lead a good case could be made for playing on any of the four suits at trick 2. It tends to be easier to plan high-level contracts than part-scores because there are usually fewer imponderables. All you can do with (b) is fiddle around and see what turns up. There is no point in worrying about it!

(c)
♠ A Q
♡ A 8 4 3
♢ K 10 8 2
♣ A 8 7

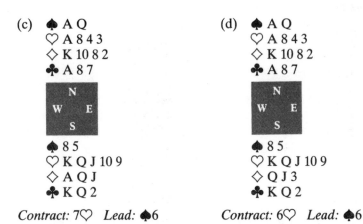

♠ 8 5
♡ K Q J 10 9
♢ A Q J
♣ K Q 2

Contract: 7♡ *Lead:* ♣6

(d)
♠ A Q
♡ A 8 4 3
♢ K 10 8 2
♣ A 8 7

♠ 8 5
♡ K Q J 10 9
♢ Q J 3
♣ K Q 2

Contract: 6♡ *Lead:* ♣6

Playing (c) do you finesse the ♠Q? Try counting top tricks. You can make 13 tricks as soon as you grasp the lead. There are no entry problems, so you must rise with the ♠A.

Now consider (d). It looks so similar, but appearances are deceptive. The *timing* of the play has been altered. This time you must lose the lead to the ♢A before you can discard your spade loser, so rising with the ♠A won't work. You must finesse the ♠Q at trick 1.

With hand (d) you have 12 potential winners (the ♠A, 5 hearts, 3 diamonds once the ♢A is driven out, and 3 clubs). You also have 2 potential losers (the ♢A and a spade). Whenever the total of winners and losers comes to more than 13 the number of tricks makeable depends on *timing*. The hand then becomes a race between declarer's winners and the defenders' ability to exploit declarer's losers. Frequently the opening lead is crucial. Here, with 12 winners and 2 losers, the total is 14 and the defenders have hit the jackpot with the ♠6 lead, giving them the edge in the race. Your 12 winners are an illusion, forcing you back onto the spade finesse at trick 1. If that fails, you are helpless.

Quiz 14

1) ♠ 6 5 3 2
♡ A Q
♢ K J 8
♣ A J 8 7

```
    N
W       E
    S
```

♠ K Q J 10 7
♡ J 7
♢ A Q 3
♣ K Q 2

i)   *Contract: 6♠   Lead: ♡5*
ii) *Contract: 6♠   Lead: ♢4*
iii) *Contract: 6♠   Lead: ♠A*
     followed by the ♡5.

2) ♠ 3 2
♡ Q 4 2
♢ A Q J 8 2
♣ 10 9 5

```
    N
W       E
    S
```

♠ A K
♡ K J 3
♢ K 10 4
♣ Q J 8 7 6

Contract: 3NT   Lead: ♠Q

3) ♠ 3 2
♡ A Q 7 6
♢ 9 7 6
♣ K Q 8 7

```
    N
W       E
    S
```

♠ K Q J 10 9 8 5 4
♡ 2
♢ A 8 5
♣ 3

i)   *Contract: 4♠   Lead: ♢K*
ii) *Contract: 3♠   Lead: ♢K*
iii) *Contract: 4♠   Lead: ♡4*

4) ♠ A Q
♡ 8 5 4
♢ K Q J 10
♣ A 7 5 4

```
    N
W       E
    S
```

♠ 3 2
♡ K Q J 10 9
♢ A 4 2
♣ 9 8 3

i) *Contract: 4♡   Lead: ♠5*
ii) *Contract: 5♡   Lead: ♠5*

17.   Starting the Defence

Being declarer is fun, but on more than half of the hands you will be a defender. Defending may seem harder, but it can be just as much fun. If you defend poorly not only will you deprive yourself of much satisfaction, but your wallet will be lighter!

The techniques that create extra tricks for declarer will serve defenders equally well and that will be our starting point. However it is sensible to note the two major differences between declaring a contract and defending against the same contract.

[1]   When you are declarer you can see your partner's hand, i.e., dummy. As defender you can see one of the enemy hands, but this is generally not as helpful.

[2]   As declarer you have to make more than half of the tricks, so most of the time you (or your dummy) will have the lead. As a defender you are trying to make a smaller number of tricks so you will have fewer opportunities for controlling the play.

Defending against No-trumps

One defender *always* has the opening lead. This can be an advantage or a disadvantage. The plus side is the chance to start attacking for tricks before declarer. The minus is that this vital decision must be made before seeing dummy, often with little knowledge of partner's hand.

We start this chapter by recapping how West, as declarer, would tackle the suits below. Then we reconsider, but this time South is declarer and West is the defender on lead. Of course West, as declarer, would not be able to see the enemy hands, but we show them to illustrate our point.

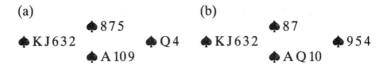

(a)   (b)
  ♠ 875   ♠ 87
♠ KJ632   ♠ Q4   ♠ KJ632   ♠ 954
  ♠ A 109   ♠ A Q 10

Playing the spades in (a) West should be conscious of the need to avoid blocking the suit, and so he would aim to play the honour from the *short* hand first. Thus, West would play a low spade to East's ♠Q, and continue spades until South takes the ♠A.

The same sequence is correct for the defenders, but now consider how this will work in practice.

(i)   West leads a low spade, but this time only *hoping* East has a spade honour. If East has just small cards in the suit, as in (b), a grateful declarer will win a cheap trick with the ♠10. Nevertheless, leading a small spade may be right more often than not.

    One further point. As declarer it wouldn't matter which small card you chose to lead, but as a defender the card chosen carries a message to partner. You don't need yet to know why. Just make a habit of *when leading a low card from a four-card or longer suit, lead your fourth-highest card of the suit:* in this case the ♠3.

(ii)   If West leads a low spade and dummy plays small, East must rise with the ♠Q.

    Admittedly declarer can almost certainly beat the ♠Q, but East is not wasting his queen. The ♠Q is being sacrificed to drive out the enemy ♠A. This might not help East to take a trick, but it promotes West's ♠ K J to winning status. Bridge is a partnership game. Each defender is part of a team. It doesn't matter who takes the tricks as long as one of you does.

    This brings us to one of the crucial guidelines of defence, namely that if your partner leads a small card, as the third hand to the trick you must play your highest card in an attempt to win the trick (or at least make the fourth hand expend as high a card as possible).

If partner leads a low card, *third hand plays high*.

(iii) Perhaps East's ♠Q will win the trick, or declarer may choose to take the ♠A and East may regain the lead later. He should not waste valuable energy wondering what to do next. Unless it is obvious that West's lead has been an unmitigated failure, and East has a good alternative idea, *East should return his partner's suit*.

To understand this vital concept, ask what are the defenders trying to achieve? They are hoping to establish and cash tricks in their longest suit. They will not gain the lead often, and if they fail to collaborate, each defender plugging away at a different suit, the odds are that the defenders will not take length tricks in any suit.

At this stage let us summarise a sequence of plays that occurs regularly, particularly when defending against no-trumps. West leads the fourth-highest from his longest suit, hoping to set up length winners. East plays 'third hand high', and returns West's suit at the first opportunity.

So if West chooses to lead a long suit, is the fourth highest always correct? Consider layout (c) with West as declarer in a no-trump contract. Of course, if West has sufficient entries to dummy he will choose to lead hearts twice from the East hand, but without sufficient entries it will be necessary to start with an honour card from his hand.

(c)   (d)

♡874   ♡87

♡KQJ32   ♡95   ♡KQJ32   ♡A4

♡A106   ♡10965

Now consider the same layout, but South is declarer and West has the opening lead. With so little information West cannot sensibly seek East's entries, so West starts with the ♡K.

If you have at least three of the top five honours in a suit, including at least two touching honours, it usually pays to lead an honour. It is then correct, for information purposes, to lead the top of your sequence of touching honours.

Thus the ♡K tells partner you don't have the ♡A, but that you possess the ♡Q and either the ♡J or the ♡10.

Please note that this strategy is correct only in as far as it works more often than not. Seeing all four hands in layout (d) it is obvious that West does best to start with a low heart, but nobody could possibly blame West for leading the ♡K, even though it fatally blocks the suit. Defending is difficult, and the secret of a successful partnership is the realisation that nobody always gets it right. Partner is trying hard!

Passive Defence

Clearly leading the ♡K from ♡ K Q J 3 2 is ideal against no-trumps, in that you combine the attack on winners with considerable safety.

Unfortunately most suits are not as solid as this, and you have already seen that leading from ♠ K J 6 3 2 can give away a cheap trick if partner has no honour in the suit. Sadly, there are many bridge players who always lead the 'fourth highest of their longest and strongest suit' even when there are ample clues that it won't work. Sometimes it is best to lead a short suit with no honours. This can work in three ways:

(i)   It is unlikely to give away a cheap trick that declarer couldn't generate otherwise.

(ii) You might just stumble on partner's long suit.

(iii) You might find yourself benefiting from a layout in which every finesse is wrong for declarer.

For example:

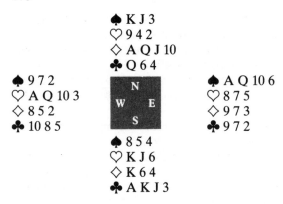

♠ K J 3
♡ 9 4 2
◇ A Q J 10
♣ Q 6 4

♠ 9 7 2
♡ A Q 10 3
◇ 8 5 2
♣ 10 8 5

♠ A Q 10 6
♡ 8 7 5
◇ 9 7 3
♣ 9 7 2

♠ 8 5 4
♡ K J 6
◇ K 6 4
♣ A K J 3

If West leads a heart against 3NT declarer easily makes nine tricks. If instead West tries a spade, declarer loses the first eight. East wins the spade lead as cheaply as possible, and switches to a heart. West wins cheaply and reverts to spades. Beautifully sadistic!

This sort of position is well known. West leads spades *through the enemy strength, up to East's strength and declarer's weakness.* East returns hearts *up to dummy's weakness.*

You must listen sensitively to the bidding. Even then the decision of what to lead might be very close.

[1] If your partner has bid a suit, you should normally lead that suit. Partner may have entered the bidding primarily to help you find the best lead.

[2] If the opponents have bid your suit the chance of establishing it is much reduced. Unless the suit is very solid, choose something else.

[3] It is more attractive to lead from a broken 5-card suit than from a similar 4-card suit. The risks of squandering a cheap trick may be the same, but the potential rewards are greater.

[4] It is more attractive to lead a long suit when you have entry cards, either outside aces and kings or the ace of your suit.

Clearly you will sometimes end up leading from a short suit, and partner will need to be able to interpret your card.

(i)   If you lead from a 3-card suit to an honour lead the bottom card. Thus if you lead from ♣ K 8 2 lead the ♣2.

(ii)   If you lead from a 3-card holding with two touching honours, lead the high honour. From ♣ Q J 4 lead the ♣Q.

(iii)   If you lead from a doubleton, lead the higher card. Lead the ♠ 8 from ♠ 8 3, or the ♠Q from ♠ Q 3.

(iv)   If you lead from a suit with three small cards, lead the middle card. The next card you play in the suit will be your highest, followed finally by the lowest. This sequence distinguishes a tripleton from a doubleton, and is described by the name MUD (short for Middle, Up, Down).

    Lead the ♣7 from ♣ 9 7 3 and follow up with the ♣9.

Note the implication of these guidelines is that the lead of a low card (2, 3, 4 or 5) tends to suggest an honour or length. The 2 usually shows a 4-card suit. The 3 suggests a 4-card or 5-card suit, depending on who has the 2.

Conversely, a middle card (6, 7, 8 or 9) often indicates a poor holding. Please note, however, that this is not an infallible rule. Whether a card is low or high depends on the bidding and other cards on view. If partner leads the ♣6, dummy has the ♣ 5 3 and you have the ♣ 4 2, partner's ♣6 is probably his fourth highest. Conversely, the ♣5 can clearly be a 'middle' card if the ♠ 8 7 6 are on view, but you can't see the ♠ 4 3 2.

Defending Against a Suit Contract

Much of the theory that you have learned about defending against no-trumps still applies. However, if the opponents have had a sensible auction which makes it clear they have a sound trump suit your priorities change.

[1]   If you are defending against no-trumps an attacking lead from a broken suit like ♡ K J 6 3 2 might gain you several length tricks if it works. But if your opponents have chosen a sensible trump suit it is most unlikely that there will be more than two heart tricks before declarer or dummy can trump, and the equation of risk against potential reward has now turned against you. Therefore fourth-highest leads from broken suits are to be avoided.

[2]   You should almost never underlead aces against a suit contract, or for that matter cash an unsupported ace. The purpose of your ace is to kill an honour in declarer's hand. Consider the following heart layout.

	♡ Q 6 4	
♡ A 9 7 3		♡ J 10 2
	♡ K 8 5	

Declarer has a right to a trick with dummy's ♡Q, but West's ♡A should prevent South's ♡K from scoring. But if West either cashes the ♡A, or underleads it, the ♡K will provide declarer with a second trick in the suit.

[3]   You have a new type of attacking lead, from a *short suit*. If you lead a singleton (very attractive) or the top card from a doubleton (fairly attractive), partner may be able to return the suit for you to trump before declarer can draw trumps.

[4]   A trump lead, especially from a holding of two or three small cards, is usually safe, and can prevent declarer from ruffing losers in dummy. At other times the bidding may suggest that declarer will attempt to cross-ruff the hand. As you gain experience you will learn to interpret the bidding to recognise such situations.

Quiz 15

1) Below are six hands. For each one, what do you lead as West:

(i) after South's 1NT has been raised to 3NT?

(ii) after South has opened 1♡, and rebid 3NT over North's 2♢ response?

(iii) after North has opened 1♣, East has overcalled 1♢, and South's leap to 3NT ended the auction?

(iv) after South has opened 1♠ and North's 3♠ ended the auction?

a) ♠ 9 7 4
♡ K J 10 9 2
♢ Q 4
♣ 9 7 4

b) ♠ 9 7 4
♡ Q 9 6 4
♢ Q 7 4
♣ 9 7 4

c) ♠ 7 4
♡ K Q J 10 9
♢ 7 5
♣ 9 7 4 2

d) ♠ 9 7 4
♡ Q 7 6 3 2
♢ 8 4
♣ J 7 3

e) ♠ 9 7 4
♡ Q 7 6 3 2
♢ A 4
♣ J 7 3

f) ♠ A 7 4
♡ 9 7 6 3 2
♢ 8
♣ J 7 3 2

2) You are East after South's 1NT opening bid has been raised to 3NT by North. You have the ♡ 10 8. West (your partner) leads a heart, and dummy produces ♡ 7 4 3.

(i) If West led the ♡A can you say who has:
  (a) ♡K?   (b) ♡Q?

(ii) If West led the ♡K can you say who has:
  (a) ♡A?   (b) ♡Q?   (c) ♡J?

(iii) If West led the ♡Q can you say who has:
  (a) ♡A?   (b) ♡K?   (c) ♡J?

(iv) If West led the ♡2, how many hearts has declarer got?

(v) If West led the ♡5, what is the largest and smallest number of hearts that declarer could have?

3) You are East after South's 1NT opening bid has been raised to 3NT. West (your partner) leads the ♣4, and dummy plays the ♣6 from:

♠ A Q 4 2
♡ 7 6 3
♢ K 10 9 8
♣ A 6

Plan your strategy with these hands.

a)   ♠ K 7 3   b)   ♠ K 7 3   c)   ♠ K 7 3
     ♡ 9 8 5   ♡ 9 8 5   ♡ Q J 10 9
     ♢ 7 6 4   ♢ 7 6 4 2   ♢ 7 6 4 2
     ♣ K 8 7 2   ♣ K 8 7   ♣ K 2

4) You are East after South's 1♡ opening bid has been raised to 3♡. West (your partner) leads the ♠8, and dummy plays the ♠10 from:

♠ A J 10 3
♡ K J 8 2
♢ 8 5 2
♣ 9 4

Plan your strategy with these hands.

a)   ♠ K 7 5   b)   ♠ K 7 5 2   c)   ♠ K Q 7 2
     ♡ A 6 4   ♡ 7 6 4   ♡ 7 5 3
     ♢ 7 6 4   ♢ 7 6   ♢ 9 7 4
     ♣ K Q J 8   ♣ J 8 5 2   ♣ J 7 2

16. Further Defensive Principles

Defensive Skills when Declarer has the Lead

Take a pack of cards and arrange the suits as below. This is plainly not a proper deal as East has 16 cards, and everybody else only 12.

Take each suit in isolation and imagine that declarer can lead from either the South or North hand. Inevitably declarer will choose to lead from South, through West, towards North, choosing the queen, or a low card. In each case how should you, as West, defend and how many tricks can declarer then make?

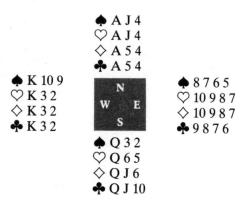

```
                 ♠ A J 4
                 ♡ A J 4
                 ◇ A 5 4
                 ♣ A 5 4
  ♠ K 10 9                      ♠ 8 7 6 5
  ♡ K 3 2         N             ♡ 10 9 8 7
  ◇ K 3 2      W     E          ◇ 10 9 8 7
  ♣ K 3 2         S             ♣ 9 8 7 6
                 ♠ Q 3 2
                 ♡ Q 6 5
                 ◇ Q J 6
                 ♣ Q J 10
```

The common theme in spades, hearts and diamonds is that if South leads the queen, you must cover with the king *promoting* a trick for the ten. You can see the point of covering in the spade suit because you have the ♠10, but it is equally true in the heart and diamond suits when East has the ten.

On the other hand if South leads a low card you should also play low, retaining your king to axe South's queen.

The purpose of an honour card is to kill opponents' honour cards.

In the club suit, covering the ♣Q with the ♣K gains nothing as South has the ♣J and ♣10, but it loses nothing either.

These examples help you understand two important guidelines:

(i) *'Cover an honour with an honour'*, the purpose being to promote a lesser card to winning status in your hand, or your partner's hand.

(ii) *'Second hand plays low'* is often contrasted with 'third hand plays high'. The difference between second and third hand is that if you are the second hand your partner still has the opportunity to stake a claim to the trick, preventing the opposition from winning a cheap trick.

The main purpose of playing 'second hand low' is to keep your honours to deal with honours in the hand sitting before you, but there is also a deceptive reason.

```
              ♠ 7 4 2
♠ Q 10 9 6 3              ♠ A 8 5
              ♠ K J
```

Suppose declarer leads the ♠2 from dummy. It might look harmless for East to grab the ♠A, after all dummy has no honour. However, declarer no longer has the losing option of trying his ♠J. If East plays low declarer might misguess.

Note that these are guidelines, not part of the laws of the game. There are exceptions, some of them obvious. For example, it would be absurd to fail to play your ace just because you happen to be the second hand if the contract is 7NT. Equally, if it is clear that it is impossible to promote anything in partner's hand there is little point in covering an honour with an honour. Layouts (a) and (b) show the potential hazards of covering. In each case North leads the ♠Q, and East must not cover with the ♠K. If East does so in (a) he crashes West's ♠A. If East covers in (b) declarer can make four spade tricks.

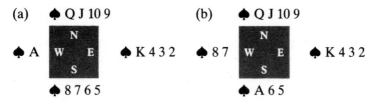

(a) ♠ Q J 10 9   (b) ♠ Q J 10 9

♠ A   ♠ K 4 3 2   ♠ 8 7   ♠ K 4 3 2

♠ 8 7 6 5   ♠ A 6 5

At this stage it is optimistic to advise you to work out exceptions, except those which are easily recognisable. Good advice is *not to cover the first of touching honours.* Suppose North has ♠ Q J 3 2 and leads the ♠Q through East's ♠K. East should not cover the ♠Q, instead saving the ♠K for the ♠J.

More on Third Hand Play

Consider East's strategy in these 'third hand' situations. In each case West leads the ♠3 against 3NT and dummy plays its lowest card.

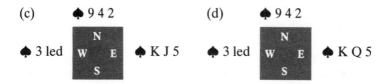

(c)   ♠ 9 4 2   (d)   ♠ 9 4 2

♠ 3 led   ♠ K J 5   ♠ 3 led   ♠ K Q 5

In (c) East should play the ♠K, not the ♠J. This is *not* a finesse position. Playing the ♠J cannot gain. If West has the ♠Q, or no honour or both honours it won't matter. However, playing the ♠J will cost a trick if declarer has the ♠Q and partner's spades are headed by the ♠ A 10.

In (d) East should play the ♠Q, the *lower* of two *touching* 'high' cards. Note the contrast with the opening leader who would lead the ♠K rather than the ♠Q from this holding. The ♠Q from third hand denies the ♠J, and makes no statement about the ♠K. Once again you cannot assume that two apparently equal cards may be interchanged at will. An expert partner will gather information from the order of cards played.

(e)   ♠ Q 6 4   (f)   ♠ Q 6 4

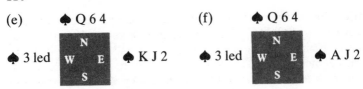

♠ 3 led   N W E S   ♠ K J 2   ♠ 3 led   N W E S   ♠ A J 2

In (e) common sense dictates that East should play the ♠J if West leads the ♠3 and dummy plays the ♠4. There is no possible circumstance where playing the ♠K is better.

Less obviously, in (f) East should also play the ♠J. Even if it loses to the ♠K, East still has the ♠A sitting menacingly over the ♠Q. Otherwise declarer will score the ♠K and ♠Q separately. You will find it helpful here to make these combinations up from a pack and experiment with holdings that declarer and West might have, consistent with the ♠3 lead. You will see that contributing the ♠J can never cost a trick.

As a general principle if you have two honours 'surrounding' dummy's honour with only one 'gap' you should consider playing the lower card.

Signalling

In our next two examples dummy plays the ♠A on West's opening ♠3 lead against 3NT. Which card should East play?

(g)   ♠ A 8 6   (h)   ♠ A 10 6

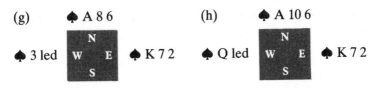

♠ 3 led   N W E S   ♠ K 7 2   ♠ Q led   N W E S   ♠ K 7 2

Obviously 'third hand high' doesn't apply here because East is not playing a card with the intention of winning the trick or driving out a higher honour. That is not a reason to relax and follow with the ♠2. West will not know that East has the ♠K, so East has a duty to impart the good news.

When a player contributes a card without hope of winning the trick the card played should be used to convey information to partner, a SIGNAL. An *unnecessarily high card* conveys the message that you like the suit partner has led. Conversely a tiny card denies interest. Therefore in (g) and (h) East should follow suit with the ♠7. If East's spades had been ♠ 7 5 2 East would have shown lack of enthusiasm with the ♠2.

Sometimes East doesn't have a card capable of sending a clear message. Change example (g) so that East has ♠ K 4 2, and so can only encourage feebly with the ♠4. West must not automatically regard the ♠4 as 'low.' An awake partner will notice that the ♠2 is missing. It would, of course, be bizarre to play the ♠K as a signal to show that you like spades; you normally SIGNAL only with cards that have no trick-taking potential. *The main purpose of a high card is to win a trick, not make a signal.*

Of course East would have to play the ♠7 from ♠ 9 7 and hope that West, examining it in the context of the other cards he can see, will not be misled.

Note the fallacy in the often-quoted theory that 'A seven or higher is a high card and encourages, while a six or lower card discourages.' You can only use the cards you were dealt. Any card should be seen as high or low *in the context of the other visible cards*.

Suppose now that West, your partner, leads the ♡A against 4♠, you see ♡ Q J 8 in dummy and you hold the ♡ 9 7. Partner would not have led an unsupported ace, so the heart layout may look like this.

                    ♡ Q J 8
♡ A K 6 4 3   ♡ 9 7
                    ♡ 10 5 2

You would like a heart ruff, so encourage with the ♡9 (just as you would have led the ♡9 from ♡ 9 7). Playing high-low with a doubleton is called a PETER.

Unblocking

In the example below West leads the ♠K against declarer's 3NT.
How do you, as East, plan to defeat this contract?

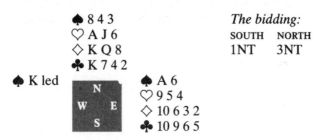

♠ 8 4 3	*The bidding:*
♡ A J 6	SOUTH NORTH
◇ K Q 8	1NT 3NT
♣ K 7 4 2	

♠ K led

East:
♠ A 6
♡ 9 5 4
◇ 10 6 3 2
♣ 10 9 6 5

West's ♠K promises the ♠Q. He should lead fourth-highest if
the ♠K and ♠Q were his only spade honours, so he will either
hold the ♠J or the ♠10. You can certainly feel pleased that you
have the ♠A to help him, but do you see the danger of automatically following suit with the ♠6? Suppose the spade layout is
as shown below.

```
               ♠ 8 4 3
♠ K Q 10 5 2               ♠ A 6
               ♠ J 9 7
```

Your ♠A will take trick 2 and you will have no spade to return at
trick 3. Declarer may then be able to take nine tricks in the other
three suits without losing the lead.

Of course it would have been easier as the cards lie if West had
started with the ♠5, but that is no excuse for blocking the suit.
You can save the day by overtaking the ♠K with your ♠A and
returning the ♠6, allowing the good guys to take the first five
tricks.

Of course things could have been worse. Exchange the South
and North hands and *unblocking* your ♠A would succeed
merely in establishing a trick for dummy's ♠J. Seeing the ♠J in
dummy you would have to follow with the ♠6, hoping that West
has a subsequent entry for his spades. Such is life!

Communications in Defence

You will be familiar with the themes demonstrated in the final two examples as we met them in chapter 15.

In the first example your ♠3 lead attracts dummy's ♠9, East's ♠K and South's ♠7. East returns the ♠6 and South plays the ♠J. How do you defend?

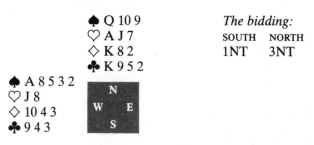

♠ Q 10 9
♡ A J 7
◇ K 8 2
♣ K 9 5 2

♠ A 8 5 3 2
♡ J 8
◇ 10 4 3
♣ 9 4 3

The bidding:

SOUTH   NORTH
1NT   3NT

If the cards are to be believed, East started with ♠ K 6 4. How would you play as declarer in 3NT with ♠ A 8 5 3 2 in an entry-less dummy opposite ♠ K 6 4? You would surely cash the ♠K and then duck a spade. Therefore in this defensive problem West must withhold the ♠A at trick 2. Hopefully East will later regain the lead and return a spade.

In our final example you choose to lead a top-of-a-sequence ♠10, won by South's ♠A. South then switches to the ♣2.

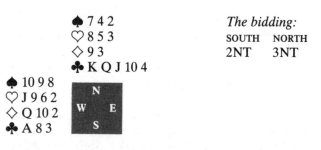

♠ 7 4 2
♡ 8 5 3
◇ 9 3
♣ K Q J 10 4

♠ 10 9 8
♡ J 9 6 2
◇ Q 10 2
♣ A 8 3

The bidding:

SOUTH   NORTH
2NT   3NT

You don't seem able to defeat declarer by active means, so as dummy has no side suit entry you had better concentrate on cutting declarer off from dummy's menacing club suit.

If South has two clubs you want to take your ♣A on the second round of the suit, but if South has three you must duck for two rounds and take the ♣A on the third round. Your partner could help you by indicating possession of two clubs or three. Normal practice is to play high-low with an even number of cards in declarer's suit, and low-high with an odd number. Partner clearly has nothing in clubs and cannot be encouraging you to lead a club.

Quiz 16

1)
    ♠ A K J
    ♡ Q 8 2
    ◇ Q J 9 2
    ♣ 7 6 2

The bidding:

SOUTH	NORTH
1NT	3NT

♠ 8 led

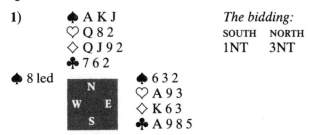

    ♠ 6 3 2
    ♡ A 9 3
    ◇ K 6 3
    ♣ A 9 8 5

West's ♠8 lead is won by dummy's ♠A. Which card should East play if declarer then leads each of the following cards:
(i)   ♡Q?   (ii) ♡2?   (iii) ◇Q?   (iv) ♣2?

2)   You are East after South's 1NT opening bid has been raised to 3NT. West (your partner) leads the ♣3, and dummy plays the ♣4 from:

    ♠ K J 7
    ♡ A 5 2
    ◇ A J 3 2
    ♣ 10 7 4

Which card do you play from these club holdings:
(a) ♣ K Q 2?   (b) ♣ A J 5?
(c) ♣ K J 5?   (d) ♣ J 9 2?

3) You are East after South's 1NT opening bid has been raised by North to 3NT. West (your partner) leads the ♣3, and dummy plays the ♣4 from:

♠ K J 7
♡ A 5 2
◇ Q J 3 2
♣ Q 7 4

Which card do you play from these club holdings:
(a) ♣ A K 2? (b) ♣ A K J?
(c) ♣ A J 5? (d) ♣ K 10 2?

4) You are East after South's 1NT opening bid has been raised by North to 3NT. West (your partner) leads the ♣8, and dummy plays the ♣A from:

♠ K J 7
♡ Q 5 2
◇ Q J 3 2
♣ A 5 4

Which card do you play from these club holdings:
(a) ♣ 10 6 3? (b) ♣ K Q 7 2?
(c) ♣ K Q 3 2? (d) ♣ K Q J 10 2?

5) You are West after South's 1NT opening bid has been passed out. You lead the ♣4 from a holding of ♣ K 8 7 4 3. Dummy plays the ♣5 from ♣ 6 5 doubleton.
(i)   If East's ♣Q wins the trick can you say who has:
(a) ♣J? (b) ♣A?
(ii) If East's ♣J loses to South's ♣A can you say who has:
(a) ♣10? (b) ♣Q?
(iii) If East's ♣10 loses to South's ♣J can you say who has:
(a) ♣9? (b) ♣Q? (c) ♣A?
(iv) If East's ♣10 loses to South's ♣Q can you say who has:
(a) ♣J? (b) ♣A?

6) West leads the ♡Q against South's 3NT. You are East.
(i) Plan the defence:
(a) If North follows with the ♡A.
(b) If North follows with the ♡5.

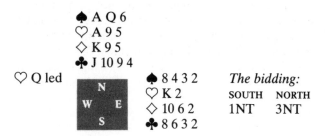

♠ A Q 6
♡ A 9 5
◇ K 9 5
♣ J 10 9 4

♡ Q led

♠ 8 4 3 2
♡ K 2
◇ 10 6 2
♣ 8 6 3 2

The bidding:

SOUTH	NORTH
1NT	3NT

(ii) Now consider the same example if instead North's hearts were ♡ A 10 5.

7) You lead the ♡5 against South's 3NT. Plan the defence in each of the following circumstances:
(i) Dummy plays the ♡4, East the ♡Q and South the ♡9. East then returns the ♡7, South following suit with the ♡10.
(ii) Dummy plays the ♡4, East the ♡10 and South the ♡Q. At trick 2 South leads the ♣K, taken by East's ♣A. East switches to the ♡7 and South follows with the ♡9.

♠ Q J 10
♡ K J 4
◇ A 8 4
♣ Q 10 5 2

The bidding:

SOUTH	NORTH
1NT	3NT

♠ 9 6
♡ A 8 6 5 2
◇ 9 5
♣ 10 6 4 3

Improving Your Game

Don't be alarmed by the heading. We are not proposing to launch you on a rigorous course of further study. You have learned the game with a view to having fun, after all, and if you want to stop reading and start enjoying yourself at this point that is fine with us. Having absorbed the contents of this book, you already know enough to play an intelligent game, and that is more than can be said for many bridge players.

However, bridge is a game that can give pleasure and satisfaction at many different levels. As your standard of play improves, the pleasure becomes more intense and the satisfaction more complete. A few words of advice for those who wish to make real progress may therefore not be out of place.

By definition, a beginners' book is limited in scope. We have examined only the basic structure of bidding and the fundamentals of play and defence. There is a great deal more to learn.

We have taught you the Acol bidding system. Playing Acol, you can be sure of finding a like-minded partner in any part of the country. As you widen your circle of bridge acquaintances, however, you will come into contact with other systems and new conventions. Do not be intimidated, and do not let anyone pressurise you into playing a convention that you do not fully understand. Tell your prospective partners that you play Acol with a weak no-trump and Blackwood, and you will find that they will be happy to accomodate you.

As you improve you might like to take time to study new conventions, and advanced techniques in bidding and card play. For now the important thing is that you have a sound foundation on which to build.

Learn From Your Mistakes

It is rare for an expert to sit through a session of bridge without making a number of mistakes. As a beginner, you must expect to make between fifty and one hundred mistakes in the course of an evening's play. There is nothing shameful about this. It is only by making mistakes that you can gain the experience needed to improve your game. What you must try to avoid, however, is settling into a comfortable rut and committing the same errors over and over again. You can do this only by facing up to your errors and attempting to put a finger on the cause. When something goes wrong, either in the bidding or the defence, make a point of discussing the matter with your partner after the game. If you can identify the bid or play that was responsible for the poor result, you will be half-way towards preventing a repetition. Don't be too ready to reproach your partner, for you will seldom be completely blameless yourself. The most rapid improvement is likely to be made by those who are willing to take most of the blame for a mishap on their own shoulders.

Bridge is so full of challenging mysteries that its allure can never fade. We have been playing the game for many years, but we expect to learn something new every time we sit down at the table.

Choose Your Company

One of the quickest ways of improving your game is by playing as often as possible with better players. Do not stray too far out of your class, for that could be damaging both to your morale and to your pocket. But if you consistently seek the company of those whom you judge to be a little better than yourself, your progress should be rapid. Don't hesitate to ask advice about any points that may puzzle you. Most players will be delighted to help. At the same time, don't accept as gospel all the advice that is showered upon you. Many players have fixed ideas that are not altogether sound.

When you cannot raise a game, you may learn something by watching at an expert table. To get the most out of this exercise, position yourself behind one player so that you can see only his cards. Try to figure out the reasoning behind his bids and plays, and ask yourself if you would have taken the same action.

If, like so many others, you become a bridge fanatic you might like to seek out a bridge club. Not only will this help your game improve rapidly, but you will quickly make many like-minded friends. Every country has a national body which will be delighted to help you find a local club. In England, contact the English Bridge Union at Broadfields, Bicester Road, Aylesbury, Bucks HP19 3BG. Most clubs play duplicate bridge, and you would be well advised to find out the differences between rubber and duplicate bridge before your first visit to a session of duplicate. Duplicate bridge can be even more addictive than rubber bridge!

A Word About Partners

A lesson that needs to be learned quickly is that all partners react unfavourably to criticism. Some tend to snap and snarl, others to brood and sulk. In either case the usual result is that the criticised partner makes a mess of the next hand as well as the last one.

As for partners who criticise you, well, you must try to put up with them. Draw partner's fangs by apologising profusely for any error, even if you feel he was in the wrong. It is a sign of good temperament if your shoulders are broad enough to bear the blame.

Finally, enjoy your bridge, win or lose.

Appendix 1.   The Stayman Convention

When describing responses to 1NT on pages 35 and 36 we saw that if responder has a 6-card major suit he has found with certainty an 8-card major fit, and with a 5-card major and game values he can jump to 3♡ or 3♠ to seek 3-card support. However none of this helps us uncover a 4–4 fit.

To solve this problem we can give up the use of a 2♣ response as a sign-off and give it an artificial use, called the Stayman convention.

(a)	♠ K J 7 3	(b)	♠ K J 7 3	(c)	♠ K J 7 3
	♡ 7		♡ 7		♡ 7
	◇ A Q 6 2		◇ A Q 6 2		◇ A 9 6 2
	♣ K 10 4 2		♣ J 10 4 3		♣ J 10 4 3

Suppose your partner opens 1NT and you hold hand (a). If a spade 4–4 fit exists you would certainly prefer 4♠ to 3NT, providing protection against enemy hearts and allowing you to score extra tricks by ruffing. If there is no such fit you would rather settle for 3NT than climb to 5♣ or 5◇. You respond 2♣, promising at least one 4-card major and asking whether partner has one. He rebids as follows:

2◇ [C] denies four cards in either major suit.
2♡ shows four hearts, possibly also four spades, as with both majors he rebids 2♡.
2♠ shows four spades, denying four hearts.

You will raise 2♠ to 4♠, or over a 2◇ or 2♡ rebid you settle for 3NT. Note that if he has four cards in each major he will remove 3NT to 4♠. Your 2♣ promises a 4-card major, and if you don't like hearts you must have spades.

You can use Stayman 2♣ with hand (b), settling for 2NT [I] if the rebid is 2◇ or 2♡. That shows the 11–12 points an immediate 2NT would have promised. You must pass 1NT with (c) because a 2♡ rebid would leave you in trouble. To use Stayman, you must be prepared for any answer.

Appendix 2.   Scoring Tables

BELOW THE LINE TRICK SCORE

For each trick over six

bid and made:	UNDOUBLED	DOUBLED	REDOUBLED
(i) in clubs or diamonds:	20	40	80
(ii) in hearts or spades:	30	60	120
(iii) in no-trumps. First trick:	40	80	160
Each subsequent trick:	30	60	120

The first side to score 100 points below the line wins a game and is said to be vulnerable. Both sides start from scratch for the next game. The first side to win two games wins the rubber.

BONUSES ABOVE THE LINE

For all five trump honours in one hand:	150
For all four aces at no-trumps:	150
For four trump honours in one hand:	100

For bidding and making a

slam:	NOT VULNERABLE	VULNERABLE
Small Slam (12 tricks):	500	750
Grand Slam (13 tricks):	1000	1500

For winning the rubber in two games:	700
For winning the rubber in three games:	500
For one game in unfinished rubber:	300
For a part-score in unfinished game:	50

For making any doubled contract:	50
For making any redoubled contract:	100

Overtricks

For each overtrick:	UNDOUBLED	DOUBLED	REDOUBLED
Not vulnerable:	Trick value	100	200
Vulnerable:	Trick value	200	400

Undertricks

Tricks short:	1	2	3	4	5
Vulnerable penalty:	100	200	300	400	500

and an additional 100 for each extra undertrick.

Non-vulnerable penalty:	50	100	150	200	250

and an additional 50 for each extra undertrick.

If doubled

Vulnerable penalty:	200	500	800	1100	1400

and an additional 300 for each extra undertrick.

Non-vulnerable penalty:	100	300	500	800	1100

and an additional 300 for each extra undertrick.

If redoubled

Vulnerable penalty:	400	1000	1600	2200	2800

and an additional 600 for each extra undertrick.

Non-vulnerable penalty:	200	600	1000	1600	2200

and an additional 600 for each extra undertrick.

A SAMPLE RUBBER

(a) We make 2♠ plus an overtrick.

We have a trick score of 60 below the line for 2♠ making, and 30 bonus points above the line for the overtrick.

WE	THEY
30 (a)	
60 (a)	

(b) They make 6♣ plus an overtrick.

They have a trick score of 120 below the line for 6♣ making, 20 bonus points above the line for the overtrick, and 500 bonus points above the slam for the successful non-vulnerable slam. They are now vulnerable, and a line is drawn below their score.

WE	THEY
30 (a)	20 (b)
	500 (b)
60 (a)	120 (b)

(c) They bid 3NT, are doubled and fail by three tricks.

Their failure costs them 800. This is scored as bonus points above the line on our side.

WE	THEY
30 (a)	20 (b)
800 (c)	500 (b)
60 (a)	120 (b)

(d) We bid 1♠ doubled and redoubled and made with an overtrick.

We score 120 below the line for 1♠ redoubled, 100 above the line for making a redoubled contract and 200 for a redoubled non-vulnerable overtrick. We become vulnerable and the score is ruled off again.

WE	THEY
30 (a)	40 (b)
800 (c)	500 (b)
100 (d)	
200 (d)	
60 (a)	120 (b)
120 (d)	

(e) We make 2NT doubled plus an overtrick.

We score 140 below the line for 2NT doubled, 50 above the line for making a doubled contract, and 200 for the doubled, vulnerable overtrick. We have scored the second game and have won the rubber by two games to one, earning the 500 rubber bonus above the line.

WE	THEY
30 (a)	40 (b)
800 (c)	500 (b)
100 (d)	
200 (d)	
200 (e)	
50 (e)	
500 (e)	
60 (a)	120 (b)
120 (d)	
140 (e)	

TOTALS   2200   660

2200 − 660 = 1540, rounded to 1500.

a) ...T.
b) Open 1◇. Rebid 1NT over 1♡ or 1♠ and 2NT over 2♣.
c) Open 1◇. Rebid 3NT over 1♡, 1♠ or 2♣.
d) Open 1NT. More descriptive than 1◇ and rebidding 2◇.
e) Open 1NT.
f) Open 1◇, the lower of touching 4-card suits with a balanced hand. Rebid 2NT over 1♠ or 3NT over 2♣.
g) Open 1♡. Rebid 2◇ over 1♠ or 2♣.
h) Open 1♡. Rebid 2♡ over 2♣ or 2◇. You are not strong enough for a 2♠ rebid, unless partner bids spades.
i) Open 1♡, the higher of 5-card suits. Rebid 2◇.
j) Open 1♡. Rebid 2♣ over 1♠ or 2♡ over 2◇. You are too weak to rebid 3♣ over 2◇.
k) Open 1♠. Rebid 2♡ over 2♣ or 2◇.
l) Open 1♡. Rebid 2♡. You are too weak to rebid 2♠.
m) Open 1◇, the middle of three touching suits. Rebid 2♣ over 1♠.
n) Open 1◇. With a red suit singleton open the suit below the singleton. Rebid 1♠ over 1♡.
p) Open 1♣. Rebid 1♡ over 1◇.

Answers to quiz 2

1) (a) No bid. No prospect of game opposite 12–14 HCP.
    (b) 2NT [I]. Opener will bid 3NT if maximum.
    (c) 3NT [S]. Even if opener is minimum you want to be in game.
    (d) 2♡ [S]. Should lead to several more tricks than 1NT.
    (e) 4♡ [S]. You know of at least an 8-card heart fit and have enough for game.
    (f) 3♡ [GF]. Opener will rebid 3NT with a doubleton heart, otherwise he will raise to 4♡.

2) (a) (i)   Pass. 2♡ was a sign-off.
        (ii) Pass. You are minimum for 1NT.
        (iii) 4♡, with 3-card support. 3♡ is game-forcing.

  (iv) Pass. 3NT is a sign-off.

  (v) Pass. 4♡ is a sign-off.

 (b) (i) Pass, though partner will love your support.

  (ii) 3NT. You are maximum for 1NT.

  (iii) 4♡. With relish! (iv) and (v) Pass.

 (c) (i) Pass. (ii) 3NT. (iii) 3NT.

  (iv) and (v) Pass.

Answers to quiz 3

1) (a) (i) 2NT [L] or 3♣ [L].

  (ii), (iii) and (iv) 2NT [L].

 (b) (i), (ii) and (iii) 1♠ [WR] [F]. Show your 4-card major. (iv) 3♠ [L].

 (c) (i) 1♢ [WR], [F]. Bid your longer suit.

  (ii) 1♡ [WR], [F]. Look for the major suit fit before agreeing the minor. (iii) 2♡ [L].

  (iv) 1NT [L]. Rather weak for 2♢.

 (d) (i) 1♢ [WR], [F]. (ii) 1♡ [WR], [F].

  (iii) 3♡ [L]. (iv) 2♢ [WR] [F1R]. This time you are strong enough to change suit at the 2-level.

 (e) (i) 2♢ [GF], showing at least 16 points.

  (ii) Help! You have the strength for a jump shift, but in which suit? Your only 4-card or longer suit is diamonds, and any diamond bid would be a limit bid, showing a far weaker hand than this. There is no 'correct' answer, a state of affairs that thankfully is not uncommon in bridge. Isn't that why the game is so fascinating? We would improvise 2♣ [WR], [F1R], but if you voted for 3NT or 3♣ you can feel that your answer was sensible. When in doubt improvise a minor suit rather than a major.

  (iii) and (iv) 3♢ [GF].

 (f) (i) and (ii) 1♠ [WR], [F].

  (iii) 2♡ [L]. (iv) 2♠ [L].

 (g) (i) 1♡ [WR], [F]. The higher of 5-card suits.

  (ii) 1♡ [WR], [F]. Look for the major fit.

  (iii) 4♡ [L]. You have an excellent fit.

  (iv) 1NT [L]. Bid cautiously with a misfit.

 (h) (i) and (ii) 1♡ [WR], [F].

    (iii) 3♡ [L].   (iv) 3♠ [L].
(j) (i) and (ii) 1♡ [WR], [F].   (iii) 4♡ [L].
    (iv) 1NT [L]. Not pleasant, but the least ugly alterna-
    tive with a horrible misfit.

2) (a) (i) Pass. Game is unlikely.
        (ii) 4♠ [S]. You have enough for game.
        (iii) Pass. Don't forget responder could have a void
        or singleton spade, so 2♠ would be unwise.
        (iv) 3NT [S], a common sense bid.
    (b) (i) 3◇ [I], a trial bid, inviting game in spades.
        3♠ is a slightly inferior alternative.
        (ii) 4♠ [S].   (iii) 2◇ [WR], [NF].
        (iv) 3◇ [WR], [F]. Hoping for 3♠ which you will
        raise to 4♠.
    (c) (i) 4♠ [S].   (ii) 4♠ [S], or even a slam.
        (iii) 3♠ [NF] [I]. Partner will bid game unless he has
        a misfitting minimum.   (iv) 4♠ [S].

Answers to quiz 4

    (a) (i), (ii) and (iii)   Rebid 2◇ [L]. You might reasonably
        have opened 1NT, but are far too weak for a 1NT
        rebid.
    (b) (i) and (ii) Rebid 1NT [L].   (iii) Rebid 2NT [L].
    (c) (i), (ii) and (iii)   Rebid 2◇ [L].
    (d) (i), (ii) and (iii)   Rebid 3◇ [L].
    (e) (i) Rebid 1♠ [WR], [NF].   (ii) Rebid 2♠ [L].
        (iii) Rebid 2◇ [L]. Not strong enough for 2♠.
    (f) (i) Rebid 1♠ [WR], [NF].   (ii) Rebid 3♠ [L].
        (iii) Rebid 2♠ [F], by-passing 2◇ and therefore
        showing a strong hand with at least 5 diamonds.
    (g) (i) 3♡ [L].   (ii) 1NT [L].   (iii) 2NT [L].
    (h) (i) and (ii) 2♣ [WR], [NF].
        (iii) 3♣ [L] or even 4♣ [L] in view of the fit.
    (j) (i) and (ii) 2♣ [WR], [NF]. You have plenty to spare,
        but you need more than this to jump to 3♣ [GF].
        (iii) 4♣ [F]. You have an excellent fit.

Answers to quiz 5

Note that these answers give *intelligent* suggestions. Some are borderline, and we would not quarrel with alternatives.

(a) (i) Pass. (ii) 2♡. This isn't a strong bid. You simply prefer hearts to diamonds.

(iii), (iv), (v) and (vi) Pass.

(b) (i) 3NT. Your 12 points opposite his 15–16 should be enough for game.

(ii) 3♡. Preference but with a jump, showing 10–12 points.

(iii) 3♡. Invites him to proceed to 4♡ unless absolutely minimum. His 2♡ rebid guarantees five hearts.

(iv) 3♠. Again you invite game.

(v) 3NT is sensible. (vi) 4♠.

(c) (i) 3NT. (ii) 2NT. 10–12 HCP and a club stopper.

(iii) and (iv) Pass. Unlikely to be enough for game.

(v) 3NT. (vi) 4♠.

(d) (i) 2♠ [S]. (ii) and (iii) 2♠. Weak hand, good suit. (iv) Pass. (v) 3♠, or perhaps 4♠ because of good playing strength. (vi) 4♠. You have a very good fit.

(e) (i) 4♠. (ii) and (iii) 3♠ [NF] [I].

(iv), (v) and (vi) 4♠.

Answers to quiz 6

1) (a) Open 2NT. The spades are too poor for an Acol 2♠.

(b) Open 2♣, and rebid 2NT [L] [NF] over 2◇ [C].

(c) Open 2♠, and rebid 3♡ [NF] over 2NT [C].

(d) Open 2♣, and rebid 2♠ [GF] over 2◇ [C].

(e) Open 2♠, and rebid 3♠ [NF] over 2NT [C].

(f) Open 1♠. There is no suitable two-level opening bid available. The spades are too poor for an Acol 2♠.

2) (a) (i) 3NT. (ii) 2NT. (iii) Pass.

(b) (i) 3♠. Opener will support spades with 3-card support and otherwise rebid 3NT.

(ii) 2♠. Then support hearts on the next round unless partner supports spades.

(iii) 4♡. 3-card support, plus an ace should make game worthwhile.

(c) (i) 3NT. (ii) 3♣. Natural.
(iii) 4♡. Opener has at least 6 hearts.

Answers to quiz 7

1) (a) 5♡. Two aces. (b) 5◇. One ace.
(c) 5♠. Three aces. (d) 5♣. No ace.
2) (a) 4◇. A cue bid, showing the ◇A or a diamond void, co-operating in case partner wants a slam.
(b) 4♠. You have shown your values with your positive response to 2♣, and don't have a side suit ace to cue-bid. Partner may well bid on towards a slam anyway.
3) (a) Pass. You are minimum for your jump shift.
(b) 5♣. A cue bid. If partner can cue-bid 5◇ a slam should be a good proposition.
(c) 4NT, Blackwood. If partner has three aces you will try 6♡.

Answers to quiz 8

1) (a) (i) 3♠. You have about 6 tricks. (ii) Pass.
(b) (i) and (ii) 1♠. The hand is strong enough for a one-level opening, and besides, the spades are too weak for a pre-emptive opening.
2) (a) 4♡. His seven tricks and your three make ten. It is best to play in the pre-emptor's long suit.
(b) 4♡. This will probably make, and more to the point, it is very likely that your opponents can make 4♠.
(c) 6♡. He has seven tricks and you have five.

Answers to quiz 9

1) (a) (i) 1♠. (ii) Pass. Clearly misfits abound.
(iii) Pass, or perhaps 2♠.
(b) (i) Pass. The diamonds are rather weak for 2◇.
(ii) Double, for takeout. (iii) Pass.
(c) (i), (ii) and (iii) Pass.
(d) (i) and (ii) 1NT. (iii) Double, for penalties.
(e) (i) 2♠, showing a strong hand and a good 6-card suit.
(ii) Pass, or perhaps 1NT. (iii) Double.
(f) (i) Pass. (ii) Double, for takeout. (iii) Pass.

2) (a) (i) 3♠ [L] [NF].   (ii) 3♣ [NF], 8–12 points.
       (iii) 3NT [S]. Partner has 16–18 points.

   (b) (i) 4♠ [S]. You have an excellent fit. Perhaps you can make 4♠ and they can make 4♡.
       (ii) 2♠ [NF], 8–12 points.
       (iii) 3♠ [GF], showing exactly five spades as would 3♠ opposite a 1NT opening bid.

   (c) (i) Pass. Be pessimistic with a misfit.
       (ii) 1NT [L], showing 6–10 points and good heart stoppers. 2♣ wouldn't be unreasonable.
       (iii) 3NT [S]. There is no point looking for 4♡ when an opponent has announced a heart suit.

   (d) (i) Pass.   (ii) 2♢. Not 1NT which shows 6–10 points.   (iii) Pass.

   (e) (i) and (ii) 4♠. Pre-emptive.   (iii) 2♠ [S].

   (f) (i) Pass. A gross misfit.
       (ii) Pass. A rare opportunity to pass a takeout double. You are making a positive decision to make hearts trumps, and expect a sizeable penalty.
       (iii) 3NT. There are a lot of hearts in this pack! As partner has the hearts guarded he presumably has the ♡A, so hearts should provide six tricks. 4♡ is a reasonable alternative.

3) (a) (i) Redouble. You would welcome a chance to double 1♠ or 2♢, and hope partner can double 2♣.
       (ii) 4♠. You have an excellent fit.
       (iii) and (iv) Double, for penalties.

   (b) (i) 1♠. Bidding naturally over the double.
       (ii) 3♠. Bid aggressively with a good fit.
       (iii) Pass. A bit weak for a penalty double.
       (iv) Pass. Nothing to say.

   (c) (i) 3♡. Bid aggressively with a good fit.
       (ii) 3♠.   (iii) 2♡. *Not* a penalty double.
       (iv) 2♡. Nearly strong enough for a penalty double.

Answers to quiz 10

1) (a) You cannot make any spade tricks.
   (b) You can make one heart trick, independently of the

distribution of the missing cards, but first you must drive out the ♡ A K Q, losing the lead 3 times.

(c) You can make 2 tricks without worrying about the missing diamonds, again losing the lead 3 times.

(d) You can make 4 tricks if the missing spades break 3–3, losing the lead once on the way. If they break 4–2 you can make 3 tricks, losing the lead twice.

(e) You can make 5 tricks if the missing hearts break 3–2, losing the lead once. Alternatively, if they break 4–1 you make 4 tricks after giving up the lead twice.

(f) You can make all 6 diamond tricks without needing to lose the lead if diamonds break 3–2. If they are 4–1 you must give up a trick in order to make 5 tricks.

(g) You can make 5 tricks provided the missing spades don't break 4–0. If they are 4–0 you must concede a trick in order to make four.

(h) You can make 5 tricks without losing the lead if hearts break 2–2. If they are 3–1 give up a trick to make 4.

(j) You can make 4 tricks if diamonds break 2–2, giving up the lead once. If they are 3–1 you make 3 tricks after losing the lead twice.

Note that in (d), (e), and (f) it is correct to play the king first. Start by cashing the high cards from the *shorter* holding to avoid blocking the suit.

2) You have 7 top tricks, the ♡ A K Q, ◇ A K and ♣ A K. You must not cash them, otherwise you will end up losing the last 6! Instead you must immediately set about developing the 2 extra tricks you need from spades. Every time you regain the lead, fire back a spade.

3) You have 8 top tricks, and the ninth will have to come from the club suit. Take your ◇Q and attack clubs. If they break 2–2 your opponents will only be able to take 2 club tricks, despite possessing the 4 top honours.

4) You have 9 top tricks: the ♠A and 4 in each red suit. Take them and ensure your contract. If you greedily try to develop club tricks you could well find grateful opponents adding 4 spade tricks to the ♣A, thus defeating 3NT.

5) This time you have only 8 top tricks: the ♠A, 3 hearts and 4 diamonds. Having taken the ♠A you have no choice but to dislodge the ♣A. If you are lucky the enemy spades will break 4–4, permitting them to take no more than the ♣A and 3 spade tricks. Otherwise you will fail in your contract, *but then there was nothing you could have done about it.*

Answers to quiz 11

1) (a) You can make 2 tricks if West has the ♠Q. Lead the ♠2 from South, and play dummy's ♠10 if West plays low. If that wins the trick, or if it loses to the ♠A you can repeat the manoeuvre, leading up to dummy's ♠J.
   Note that playing the ♠K on the first round may score you a quick trick if West has the ♠A and East the ♠Q, but it won't help you develop a second trick in the suit. In this example the position of the ♠A is almost immaterial. It is the ♠Q that matters.

   (b) You can make 2 tricks if West has the ♡Q, or ♡K, or both. Lead the ♡2 to dummy's ♡10. This will probably lose to East's honour, but provided West has the remaining honour a subsequent finesse of the ♡J will be successful.

   (c) This time there is no point in leading the ♢J, *because you don't have the ♢10.* The correct play is to cash dummy's ♢ A K and lead the ♢2 towards your ♢J. You will make three tricks by a finesse if *East* has the ♢Q. Alternatively, if West has the doubleton or tripleton ♢Q you will make a third trick by brute force or length.

2) You have 8 top tricks. A heart finesse could provide a ninth, but once the ♠A is gone you have no spade stopper. Whether you risk this finesse or not depends on your requiring the extra trick for your contract.
   (i) Needing only 8 tricks, take no risks.
   (ii) Now you need a ninth trick so finesse the ♡Q.

3) To make your slam you need three tricks from the club suit. If clubs break 3–2 any line of play will succeed, but if either

defender has a singleton ♣K, or East has ♣ K 10 9 8 you will need to cash the ♣ A and lead from dummy towards your two remaining honours.

Answers to quiz 12

1) You can count only 10 winners (the ♠A, 6 diamonds and 3 clubs). A heart ruff in dummy will provide the eleventh so win the ♠A and prepare the ground by returning a heart.

2) This time you abandon the idea of drawing trumps altogether in favour of a cross-ruff. You can practically ensure 10 tricks by taking the ♢A, cashing two black suit aces and cross-ruffing spades and clubs, backwards and forwards.

3) You must plan to increase your total of winners to 13 by establishing 3 club length winners in dummy, but you will need the ♠A as an entry. Win the ♢A, cash the ♠ K Q, take dummy's ♣ A K and ruff the ♣ 2. If the clubs have broken 3–2 dummy's clubs are now winners, so you can enter dummy with the ♠A and cash the ♣ 8 5 3.

   If spades had broken 3–1 you would have had to play identically, even though that would have involved cashing the ♣ A K before drawing the last trump.

4) You seem to have one loser in each suit. This is a hand where you have urgent business to attend to, so drawing trumps must wait. Win the ♡A and immediately play a diamond, allowing you to discard your heart loser on the ♢K as soon as the defenders force out your ♡K.

5) The ♣K lead has left you with an immediate club loser, and you cannot avoid losing a trick to the ♠A. Win the ♣A, cash the ♢ A K, enter dummy with the ♡A and throw the ♣4 on the ♢Q. Now you can drive out the ♠A.

6) You seem to have far too many losers in your hand to even contemplate a grand slam, but if you start ruffing diamonds in dummy you will find that you can establish length winners. Try the following sequence:

   Take the ♢A, ruff the ♢2, return to your hand with the ♡A and ruff the ♢3. If diamonds have broken 3–3 all your diamonds are winners so you can draw trumps, but we will assume a 4–2 diamond break. Re-enter your hand with the ♣A to ruff the ♢5. Finally trump a heart and draw trumps. The ♢8 and ♢7 are now winners.

Answers to quiz 13

1) Both a count of winners (12 only if you include 6 trump tricks) and losers (a club and possibly the ♠K) make it clear you cannot afford a trump loser. You may need two entries to dummy to finesse spades, and these must come from the heart suit. Therefore win the ♣A, cross to dummy by overtaking the ♡10 with the ♡J (not the ♡K) and finesse the ♠Q. If successful, re-enter dummy by overtaking the ♡Q with the ♡K for a second spade finesse.

2) You have 7 top tricks and can establish 2 extra diamond winners provided the suit breaks no worse than 4–2. But you must preserve the ♡K as an entry to your hand, so take dummy's ♡A at trick 1 and cash your diamond winners from the top, conceding the fourth round if they break 4–2.

3) You have 9 top tricks but the awkward 'blocked' diamond and heart holdings make entries to both hands potentially difficult. The play depends on which black ace the opening lead removes. Therefore:
    (i)   With the ♠A removed it is entries to dummy which concern you. Cash the ♡ A K, then the ♢ K Q and ♡ Q J. Finally return to your hand with the ♣A to cash the ♢A.
    (ii) With the ♣A removed you must be careful with entries to your hand. Cash the ♢ K Q, then the ♡ A K and ♢A. Now re-enter dummy with the ♠A to take the ♡ Q J. If you are in doubt, try alternative lines of play to see which succeeds.

4) You have plenty of winners and no loser problems, so what can go wrong? If you take the ♡K (correctly preserving the ♡A as an entry to dummy) and play the ♣Q, carelessly following with dummy's ♣2, an inspired defender might hold up, leaving you with insufficient entries to establish and

enjoy any further club trick. (Try it and see!) You would then be dependent on a friendly break in diamonds. To ensure your contract overtake the ♣Q with the ♣K, and if that holds the trick continue with the ♣J.

5) You have lots of tricks once the ◇A is dislodged, but there is a danger that the defenders will take four heart tricks when you concede the ◇A. It is worth withholding your ♡A for two rounds, in the hope that if hearts do break 5–3 or worse, the hand with the ◇A has no hearts left.

6) If clubs break 3–2, by conceding the third round of clubs you make 5 club tricks to go with the ♠ A K, ♡A and ◇A. It is not good enough to cash the ♣ A K and then give up a club, as you have no further entry to dummy. Win the ♠A and immediately concede a club.

7) It is tempting to hold up, but then a spade switch would sink you without trace. At least the hearts might break 4–4, so take advantage of your good fortune in avoiding a spade lead by winning the ♡A and driving out the ◇A.

8) You have 9 top tricks and it appears the lead has given you a free opportunity for a tenth, by means of the diamond finesse. However, beware! You have been very fortunate to avoid a heart lead, which would have prematurely removed the entry to your hand for your ♠Q. A losing diamond finesse could easily be followed by a heart switch, so rise with the ◇A and cash your ♠ A K.

Answers to quiz 14

1) (i) You have 12 winners after driving out the ♠A, but you don't have time to draw trumps and discard the ♡J on the ♣J. Therefore finesse the ♡Q.

(ii) Take the ◇A and drive out the ♠A. You should decline any subsequent heart finesse.

(iii) Now you don't need a heart finesse, so rise with dummy's ♡A and take your 12 tricks.

2) You have 7 top tricks and can develop additional tricks from clubs or hearts. Although your clubs are longer, you can

only afford to lose the lead once before you are over-whelmed in spades, therefore attack hearts.

3) (i)   You have 10 winners (7 spades once the ♠A is driven out, the ♡A, ◇A and a club) but time is against you. You also have 4 immediate losers to attend to (2 diamonds, the ♠A and the ♣A). Therefore you must win the ◇A and finesse the ♡Q in an attempt to reduce your losers to 3. If that fails you will go two off.

(ii)   The same arguments apply as in (i), but now 4 losers pose no threat so win the ◇A and get on with drawing trumps.

(iii)   This time the heart lead has removed your only entry to dummy's clubs, so you need the heart finesse.

4) (i)   You have 10 winners (the ♠A, 4 hearts once the ♡A is dislodged, 4 diamonds and the ♣A), but also 4 possible losers (the ♡A, one spade and 2 clubs). If you greedily take the spade finesse and lose to the ♠K, a club switch could remove your ♣A before you have knocked out the ♡A; therefore to ensure your contract you must rise with the ♠A and draw trumps.

(ii)   Now you need the spade finesse to bring your total of winners to 11. If it fails, a club switch restricts you to 9 tricks.

Answers to quiz 15

1) (a)   (i)   The ♡J. Top of an interior sequence.
        (ii)   The ♠7 (MUD) or perhaps ♣7. South bid hearts.
        (iii)   The ◇Q. Top-of-a-doubleton in partner's suit.
        (iv)   A spade. You don't expect to make any heart length-tricks, and a heart lead from ♡ K J 10 6 2 risks throwing a trick if declarer has the ♡Q. A trump is safe and may cut down ruffs in dummy.
   (b)   (i)   The ♠7 (or ♣7). The ♡4 is possible, but you have insufficient entries to make that attractive.
        (ii)   The ♠7 or ♣7. Definitely not a heart now.
        (iii)   The ◇4. Lowest from three-to-an-honour.
        (iv)   A spade.
   (c)   All parts lead the ♡K. Your suit is so strong.

(d) (i) The ♠7. The ♡3 isn't unreasonable, but you have no entries. If you choose a passive lead from a short suit a tripleton is better than a doubleton, and leading from ♣ J 7 3 isn't attractive.

    (ii) The ♠7. MUD

    (iii) The ♢8. Top-of-a-doubleton in partner's suit.

    (iv) The ♢8. Perhaps you may get a diamond ruff. A trump is a reasonable alternative.

(e) (i) The ♡3. This time you have an entry, the ♢A.

    (ii) The ♠7. Again, don't lead declarer's suit unless it is very strong.

    (iii) The ♢A. Top-of-a-doubleton in partner's suit.

    (iv) A spade. The ♢A is an interesting alternative. It isn't normally sensible to lead an unsupported ace against a suit contract, but it may turn out well if it leads to a ruff.

(f) (i) The ♡3. It is your longest suit.

    (ii) The ♣2. No point in leading hearts if declarer has bid the suit.

    (iii) The ♢8. It may not be right, but partner has bid diamonds so it will keep him happy.

    (iv) The ♢8. A singleton is an excellent lead against a suit contract.

2) (i) (a) West. The ♡A promises the ♡K.

    (b) You don't know. West might have led the ♡A from ♡ A K Q 6 2 or ♡ A K J 6 2.

  (ii) (a) South. The ♡K denies the ♡A.

    (b) West. The ♡K promises the ♡Q.

    (c) West. West would lead the ♡K from ♡ K Q J 6 2, but the ♡6 from ♡ K Q 9 6 2.

  (iii) (a) You don't know. West could have ♡ Q J 9 6 2 or ♡ A Q J 6 2.

    (b) South. The ♡Q denies the ♡K.

    (c) West. The ♡Q promises the ♡J.

  (iv) West has four so South has four.

  (v) The ♡5 is fourth highest. The ♡4 and ♡3 are visible. Who has the ♡2? If West has it, West has five hearts and South three. Otherwise South has four hearts.

3) Clearly you must take the ♣K (third hand high), but what then? The ♣4 is obviously fourth highest. You should be on the lookout for the ♣3 and ♣2!
(a) You have the ♣2. If partner has the ♣3 declarer has only two clubs. Otherwise declarer has three, but whichever is the case it is clearly right to return your partner's suit. Return the ♣2, your original fourth highest.
(b) Once again you should return a club, the ♣8 (next highest) being correct as you started with only three.
(c) Which card does declarer play? If the ♣3, declarer started with five clubs. Even if the ♣5 is played declarer started with four, making it unlikely that you can set up West's suit. A heart switch (the ♡Q) is more attractive.

4) The ♠8 looks like a MUD lead or perhaps a doubleton.
(a) Take the ♠K and switch to the ♣K.
(b) Again take the ♠K, and try switching to the ♢7 hoping for a ruff.
(c) The spade lead has hit the jackpot, but you will have to be patient. Take the ♠Q (lower of touching honours is correct) and switch to a passive ♢7. West will know you have the ♠K when your ♠Q takes trick 1, so on regaining the lead he can judge whether it is best to revert to spades.

Answers to quiz 16

1) (i) The ♡A. Cover an honour with an honour.
(ii) The ♡3. Second hand plays low. Save your ♡A for dummy's ♡Q.
(iii) The ♢3. Don't cover the first of touching honours. If the ♢Q wins the trick and dummy's ♢J comes next, cover it with the ♢K in case your partner has the ♢10.
(iv) The ♣5. Second hand plays low. Declarer might have the ♣K and ♣J, and will have to guess which one to play.

2) (a) The ♣Q. Third hand high, but lower of touching honours.
(b) The ♣A. Third hand high. Playing the ♣J is *not* taking a finesse.
(c) The ♣K. As with (b).
(d) The ♣9. Keep the ♣J for dummy's ♣10.

3) (a) The ♣K. Third hand high, but lower of touching honours.

    (b)   The ♣J. Common sense.

    (c)   The ♣J. The ♣A and ♣J surround dummy's ♣Q, with a gap of only one card. Keep the ♣A to deal with dummy's ♣Q.

    (d)   The ♣10. Similar to (c).

4)   (a)   The ♣3. You have no reason to encourage West to continue clubs if he regains the lead.

    (b)   The ♣7, to encourage a club continuation.

    (c)   The ♣3. You would like to express enthusiasm with a higher card, but you don't have one that you can afford.

    (d)   The ♣K. You might as well signal for a club continuation as spectacularly as you can manage.

5)   (i)   (a)   South has the ♣J. East's ♣Q denies the ♣J.

          (b)   South has the ♣A. If East had it, East would have played it to trick 1 (third hand high).

    (ii)   (a)   South has the ♣10. East's ♣J denies the ♣10.

          (b)   East has the ♣Q. If South had it South would not have needed to waste his ♣A on trick 1.

    (iii)   (a)   South has the ♣9. East's ♣10 denies the ♣9.

          (b)   South has the ♣Q. If East had it East would have played it (third hand high) rather than the ♣10.

          (c)   South has the ♣A, for the same reason as (b).

    (iv)   (a)   You don't know who has the ♣J. East would have played the ♣10 from ♣ 10 2 or ♣ J 10 2.

          (b)   South has the ♣A, as in (iii) (c).

6)   (i)   (a) and (b). West has led from a heart suit headed by ♡ Q J 10. Your ♡K blocks the suit, so jettison it now. Return the ♡2 at your first opportunity.

    (ii)   (a) and (b). West's hearts now are headed by ♡ Q J 9, and unblocking the ♡K will hand dummy a second heart trick. You can only play the ♡2 and hope.

7)   (i)   Hopefully East started with ♡ Q 7 3, and has an entry card in another suit. Withhold your ♡A at trick 2 to keep open defensive communications, following suit with the ♡2, your original fifth highest.

    (ii)   This time it looks as though East started with ♡ 10 7 3. This will be quite good enough if he regains the lead, so long as you withhold your ♡A.